We Bought The Farm!

By Peg Cleary-Osborne

ISBN-13: 978-1503061248
.

Printed in the United States of America 2014

Dedication

To My Children

Table of Contents

Acknowledgements

First and foremost, I want to thank my family. Without them there would be no story to tell. I would also like to thank our then good and helpful neighbors while we lived on the farm during those four years.

I would also like to thank several friends in the writing field; Lisa Kunzig, Pat Leali and Dijana Winter, who helped to critique my story with good suggestions and helpful advice.

Next, I would like to thank two computer gurus; Sanford Kent and Reginald Prior who were there for me when my computer failed to cooperate at times while I was writing this book.

Last and not least, I want to thank Mary Kathleen Dougherty who helped to publish the book for me and Shirley Rea who edited the book. They were very supportive in this endeavor of mine and for that, I am very grateful.

Preface

You may not call me a writer and I may not call me a writer, but I have a story to tell. Sometimes it was funny and sometimes it was sad, but always it was interesting and sometimes quite harrowing. I learned to do more with less and I found joy in simple things. OK, maybe not always joy, but there were a lot of simple things and I learned to live with them.

I thought at first it would be a neat idea to write the book for my children who were too young at the time to fully remember or even to understand all the undertakings that were involved in keeping things running while we lived on the farm. I also wanted to write about it before my brain cells began to deteriorate!

I also began to think it might be interesting and insightful for others who might have given some thought about doing the same things we did and for whatever reason didn't pursue their plans. They may now be grateful they didn't after reading this book!

Even those who have spent their whole lives living on a farm might find it interesting to read my story. I think they would enjoy sitting in their favorite armchairs while shaking their heads in amusement as they read about our episodes and compare it to their own.

Then there are those who may think it would be a wonderful idea to live on a farm and to have all the land and animals they wanted without having to be concerned about ordinances, complaining neighbors, etc., and to be able to grow all the vegetables and plants they wanted to enjoy. They may have a change of heart after reading this story.

While writing this book, it gave me a chance to remember and reminisce about all the interesting experiences that happened to my family and me. We were true greenhorns, to say the least!

This is about our experiences during those four plus years, from 1971 to 1975, as we desperately tried to keep ourselves and everything else functioning.

As I look back over that time, it seemed as though it flew by in an instant; and then again, it seemed as though those years lasted a lifetime. I met many people I would never have known otherwise and I learned a tremendous amount of things along the way. Life can be quite the fascinating journey!

Except for my son and me, names in this book have been changed to protect the innocent.

Chapter 1
How It All Began

We originally lived in a small town in Western Pennsylvania. I was then a young 33-year-old housewife; whose life I felt was quite basic with an everyday ebb and flow. I had no plans beyond that, nor did I have any idea what the future held in store for me.

When Mark told me that he was offered a promotion that would mean we had to move to upstate New York, I remember being quite excited about the new adventure ahead of us. It would be like moving to a foreign country after living in the same small town for over 30 years!

I loved the water then and still do, so the fact that we might be living near one of the Great Lakes made the move seem even more exciting. It was sad and difficult for me to leave my family and friends behind; people whom I knew and loved, but this was a chance to experience something new and exciting.

It was the month of February when the time came for us to leave Pennsylvania and look for a home in Rochester, NY. At that time of year the housing market was very limited. As diligent as we were to find a home that first week, we weren't successful. We decided by the end of the week that we would rent a place while we continued to look for a home. That way we would get to know the area better and not rush into buying something that we may regret later. At the time we had 3 daughters, and we felt it wasn't fair for them to stay with family members while we traveled back and forth from one state to another as we continued to look for a house.

Quite conveniently at the end of that week, a friend of Mark's who lived in the suburbs, informed us of a home for rent just a block down the street from where they lived. We looked at the home and decided we would rent it.

Moving day arrived a month later. Once we had moved, we did our best to settle in and discover our new surroundings. When we had free time, Mark and I would look for a house to buy.

Mark, being an avid outdoorsman, decided to get a membership to a Rod and Gun Club as soon as possible. On Sunday mornings he would travel a distance of about forty-five minutes to get to this Rod and Gun Club to shoot skeet and practice shooting with his rifle and pistol. This was a good diversion for him and it made him happy.

One morning he returned home much earlier than usual extremely upset! He blatantly announced then and there, that I should stop looking for a home to purchase in the Rochester area! We were going to buy a place somewhere else with a large amount of land so he could shoot skeet any day of the week and any time of day!

He went on to tell me that when he was shooting at the range, a man from the Club House approached him and asked him if he had a membership to shoot there. Mark said he did, so the man asked Mark to show him his membership card. When Mark gave the man his card, he looked at it and said, "This membership is for using the shooting range every day of the week except Sunday. Since this is Sunday, you can't shoot here today. However if you want to, you need to purchase a special permit to use the range on Sundays!"

Hence, the search for a home with a lot of land is where my story really begins.

Chapter 2
The Hunt Is On

M ark started to look for places on his own while I stayed home with our three daughters. Then one day he came home and asked me if I would look at a farm he saw in the Southern Tier. I agreed to go, so we made an appointment with the realtor to take us to see this farm of over one hundred and ten acres.

"This should qualify for the amount of property Mark was looking for", I thought to myself. The drive was over an hour to get to this farm and it seemed as though it was taking forever for us to get there. It was early spring and the countryside still seemed desolate with the winter snow. It seemed especially desolate where we were going because the elevation was much higher than where we were presently living, as the farm was located in the foothills of the Allegheny Mountains.

When we arrived at the farm, we met the owners. They were an older couple with an adult daughter who was also there visiting them with the intent to meet us. The wife said her husband was in the early stages of dementia and they needed to sell the home because of his health.

After meeting them, the realtor walked me through the 100-year-old home of eleven rooms. Six of the eleven rooms were bedrooms. Closets are generally unheard of in older homes, but this home not only had closets, but all the closets except for one bedroom, were the size of bathrooms! I was truly amazed at this, which for a female it just put more value towards the house!

The living room had a large picture window that overlooked a 30-mile view of rolling hills. The picture window was the only new window in the house. All the other windows were the old rippled glass from the 19th century.

A driveway encircled the house in a crescent shape. At one side of the driveway on the east side of the house, was a porch with a front door that led to a good-sized entrance room. This room had a fireplace between the front stairway and a door that led to a room that we later dubbed the TV room. There was another large doorway that led to the living room. I thought having a fireplace in an entrance room was quite quaint.

The home had two sets of staircases; one staircase in the front of the house, which as I mentioned, was located off from the entrance room, and one staircase in the back of the home off from the kitchen.

Next we walked out to the barns. There were four sheds for various purposes and a huge L-shaped two-story barn. The moment I walked in the main barn and saw a large, magnificent ceiling structure that reminded me of a wooden cathedral, I became a little giddy. I never thought in my wildest dreams we would ever be able to afford that amount of land, house, and barn structures that I was viewing!

However, as fate would have it, the owners accepted our offer, and that is when "We Bought the Farm!"

Chapter 3
This Will Be the Start of Something New

The following month we made a few trips back and forth to show our daughters the farm, discussed moving arrangements with the former owners, and measured the room sizes for decorating purposes.

Because of the altitude, there was still snow on the ground in the area. (That particular spring, the snow was still on the hillside north of town in the middle of May!) That was something unheard of where we formerly lived in Pennsylvania!

We began to notice, as the days got warmer with spring arriving, that the air was becoming more than just fresh spring air. It was the pungent smell of farm country! This fragrance was labeled "Eau de Manure". The neighbor that farmed our property proudly proclaimed when we first met him, that this county was known to have more cows than it had people!

The prior owners had bales of hay surrounding the farmhouse foundation so there would be better insulation in the winter months. Since Mark was so eager to get started with the move, he decided to volunteer to remove these cold, frozen, wet bales of hay from the foundation. This way, the former owners wouldn't need to be concerned about having to do this before they moved. Of course, this was a great family project and Mark was happy that we could all do this for the former owners!

As the trips began to increase, I started to become ill. After a phone call to the doctor, he said I probably had the flu. However, nothing he prescribed that I took seemed to help.

After six weeks of feeling crappy, the doctor said I had better come in to his office for an examination. I made the appointment and was eager to discover what remedy I could take so I could start to feel better. After all, we were in the process of moving and I needed all the strength and energy I could muster.

After the doctor finished examining me, he looked at me and said, "Congratulations! You are going to have a baby!"

In shock I asked him, "How did that happen?!" He responded, and said, "I don't know, I wasn't there!"

When the office people at Mark's work learned of the cause of my condition, they all said, "Stay away from Mark, you may get the flu!"

We weren't sure when the fourth child was due because we didn't know when THIS happened. Since we waited to move at the end of June when the girls would be out of school for their summer vacation, I was quite large in size by that time.

My family and friends lived 250 miles away and our daughters were four, ten, and eleven years old, so I was grateful some of the men from the company where Mark worked, volunteered to help us with the move!

As I mentioned before, the farmhouse had eleven rooms and six of them were bedrooms; some bedrooms were small and some were large. One bedroom in particular was quite large. At that time, it was painted an ungodly eggplant color. On moving day, when neither we nor the men helping us knew where to put a box or an item, we just said, "put it in the Purple Room!" And so it was christened. The color was never changed nor was it repainted right up to the day we moved from the farm!

The kitchen had a tremendous amount of cupboard space. One full wall from the floor to the ceiling was an old wainscot cupboard. There was also a separate floor to ceiling wainscot cupboard on an adjacent wall. As I was putting canned goods away in that particular cupboard, I discovered a small bottle of cognac hidden in a corner alcove. I had to chuckle to myself about what the story may have been behind that secret stash.

Also, in the kitchen was a small potbelly stove that the former owners must have used to heat the room. This had a pipe that went up through the kitchen ceiling through a bedroom upstairs and on to the roof. This stove was situated right next to the stove for cooking. Mark decided to remove it from the kitchen, as it wasn't safe to have the stove where a toddler would eventually be running around it. Also, the pipe would get too hot for the bedroom it was going through and it was quite the eye sore!

Later as winter set in and I needed to be in the kitchen much of the time, I realized why the former owners had the potbelly stove in the kitchen! The kitchen floor was freezing in the wintertime!!

Our youngest daughter Charlotte was known to be our 'Happy Wanderer' of the family. In the hustle and confusion of moving day, I noticed she was missing and I panicked! I had everyone stop everything to look for her inside and outside of the house but we couldn't find her anywhere! Then I decided to go up the back staircase to the Purple

Room to check that area of the house. As I got to the top of the steps, I just happened to look into the very little bedroom on the left of the staircase. Lo and behold, there was our little four-year-old daughter sound asleep on top of a very small and very uncomfortable wooden slat coffee table. We all breathed a sigh of relief and went on with our work.

As time went on, Charlotte continued to be our "Happy Wanderer". One afternoon Charlotte was missing again only to be found all the way up the back lane entertaining herself by picking burdock buds and sticking them together to make little baskets. It was innocent enough and she was puzzled why we were so upset, but it still gave us a fright when we couldn't find her.

Chapter 4
Settling In Discoveries

Once we got settled in, we discovered many things one never notices when looking for a home or property. You think you know what you want and don't want when you go to purchase a home, but you can never quite remember everything once you get caught up in the so called 'romance' of looking for a home. Yes, all of you homeowners know exactly what I'm talking about.

For example, the beautiful thirty-mile view from the picture window in the living room showed more than a view of the rolling hills after the snow melted. Surprise! Surprise! There was the town dump!!

When the realtor was showing us the house, he pointed to a room off the enclosed back porch. This enclosed back porch was formerly a washroom for farm hands when the home was newly built. He referred to it as the "Emergency Room". I remember thinking it was just another closet. However, I didn't realize until we moved in that the "Emergency Room" was actually a three-seated outhouse! And it was attached to the house! The house had so many large closets, that I just assumed it was another one!

The well water was very hard and it smelled of sulfur. The girls complained a bit about the taste and it took them some time to get used to this. After we left the farm four years later, I found it comical to hear the girls *complain* about the flavor of the water in our new home; as it no longer tasted like the sulfur water they were used to drinking.

Washing clothes? Another challenge! After doing the laundry a couple times, it was discovered that every piece of white clothing turned to a rust color because of all the iron in the well water!! Quite exasperating to say the least! Anything that was originally white had to be discarded, as bleach couldn't resolve the dilemma. When we realized this, we had to purchase a water softener so our white clothes would stay white! Once the softener was installed, the first load of white laundry came out whiter than they did before they went into the washer!

The bedrooms had no electrical outlets and there was only one light fixture in each room composed of a single light bulb in a light socket in the center of the ceiling with a drop down pull chain to turn the light on and off. When you went to bed at night, you had to grope blindly in the dark for that one and only chain that was innocently dangling from the light fixture. (Which by the way, had no light shade on it either!) This type of lighting was in every one of the six bedrooms.

As I mentioned previously, the house had two sets of staircases and both stairs had a pull chain along the side of the railing. When you needed light to go up the steps at night, you had to pull the chain for the light to go on at the landing at the top of the stairs. Once you got to the top of the stairs, you needed to pull the chain on the staircase to shut the light off.

After a few months of groping in the dark for these nightly rituals, Mark decided to have an electrician come in to install more outlets and electric light switches. He asked an electrician from where he worked to do this for us.

The first assignment the electrician tackled was to install the light switches at the top and bottom of the main staircase. While he began to do this, he learned that inside the staircase wall were eight by eight inch beams used to support the house. These beams needed to be drilled through to install the light switches! He had no tools with him for that kind of task and he lived an hour away. Instead of going back to his place for the tools that he needed, he chose to chisel out by hand what he needed to do to install the light switches. It took him eight hours to do just that one job of installing the two light switches in the main hallway steps!

Several months later there was a tremendous wind storm during the night that really concerned me, but I reminded myself that the house was being held up with those huge eight by eight beams and I was not to be concerned!

The former owner informed us of areas of the home that were important for us to know about before we moved in. I had no idea what she was talking about when she mentioned something about a cistern. She informed us that the water supply in the house was shared between a shallow well and a cistern. I didn't know what a cistern was so again, I kind of blew it off. She told us that the cold water was for drinking and that it came from the shallow well. The hot water came from the cistern and that water was to be used only for cleaning and laundry.

She went on to say, "When you use the water for drinking after you have used the hot water, you need to run the cold water for a while before you drink it." OK, whatever! I had that attitude until we moved in and company started to arrive week after week. We shall get to that part later.

Back to the cistern and the well: once we realized how shallow the well really was, and with the five of us flushing the toilet and using the water for other necessary uses, we had to call the neighbor who lived up the road from us to bring us water to keep up the well level. This neighbor had a truck with a large metal cylinder container on the back that held the water.

Of course, visitors who lived in *normal* houses weren't aware that we had to conserve as much water as possible when they had to use the facilities at our place. So every weekend after they left, we had to call the neighbor up the road to bring in more water to supply the well again.

There was one infamous weekend where the girls all needed to take a bath before they went to school the next day. After they went to bed, I wanted to take a bath also. I was then eight months along in my pregnancy.

I got into the bathtub with this huge belly with the great expectation to relax for a few minutes. In this house, there was no such thing as a shower. I turned on the water and while I was sitting there stark naked, nothing but mud flowed from the faucet onto me and into the bathtub! I couldn't help it and I began to cry. The hormones from the pregnancy, the stress of entertaining, etc., etc., just got the best of me. When Mark saw the condition I was in, he immediately called the area's well driller. He asked him if we could possibly be bumped up in line from the many customers that were on their waiting list, to "as soon-as-possible", because his wife was pregnant. The well driller accommodated us as soon as he was able, and eventually he drilled a very deep well for us with lots of water and all were happy again.

Chapter 5

Learning About the Locals

Quite unexpectedly we were introduced to our first local residents the first night we stayed at the farm.

We had just gone to sleep, when we heard a loud pop and crash, and then silence. Mark jumped out of bed and tore downstairs to see what might have happened. I was right behind him.

In the field across from our house, was a car with no headlights on. The loud noise must have been when it hit the berm of the road. When Mark looked inside and saw no one in the car, he yelled at me to call the police. While we were waiting for them to arrive, Mark walked around and found a young man sitting not far from the car. He then asked him if that was his car, which it was. Soon after the police arrived and questioned him further. They found out there were two other passengers as well as him so they started combing the field. They were surprised when they found the young men to learn they had no injuries. I guess the relaxing effect of the alcohol they all drank, saved their lives!

Unbeknownst to me at the time, there were many neighbors that weren't happy with us for buying the farm. I learned some of the local farmers wanted to purchase the farm but for whatever reasons, weren't able to do so.

The first hairdresser I went to for my haircuts told me that the village people said my husband was a doctor. Not so! Then she went on to say that they thought we came to this little god-forsaken town because we wanted to avoid 'bussing' our children. Again not so! I found it quite amusing to discover how gossip can conjure up so many different stories! How many more stories were there floating around out there?

Our first visitor happened to be our next-door neighbor who just had a high school graduation party for their oldest daughter. They brought us some graduation cake and introduced themselves to us. Later on, one of their younger daughters and our daughter Marie became very strong friends.

I was told many years later, that during the summer, Marie and her friend would sneak down to a nearby pond and watch some of the local boys go skinny-dipping!

They also liked to go fishing at that pond. When they caught a fish, they would ask our neighbor if he would take the fish off the hook and clean it for them. He seemed to be happy to do this and he chuckled at the girl's skill in fishing. There was no way I was going to do that!

I don't remember who got the fish to cook after it was cleaned; was it Marie's friend or our generous neighbor?? I don't remember cooking any fish for us and that was just fine with me. At the time, since I had yet to be introduced to how delicious fresh fish could be, I only knew of the strong flavor and odor of frozen fish. Fresh fish was not something we knew much about where we lived in western Pennsylvania.

Shortly after we moved in, another neighbor and his wife stopped by to visit us and we became good friends. They asked if they could rent our land to farm their crops and Mark consented to this.

Later on Mark and this friend and other friends came to our place every Sunday morning to shoot skeet in the back of our barn. All were happy. This farmer got quite attached to our son Tommy and our son was also quite attached to him.

Once they started to farm our land, they planted feed corn on most of the property for the animals. Then without telling us, they also planted several long rows of sweet corn at the edge of the field, close to our property for us to enjoy. That was a real treat! It was a good friendship and Mark enjoyed hunting with his friend and his friend's family. It was tough to leave them when we had to move.

Then there was a time when I needed to have some knives sharpened. I was told there was a man who lived about a mile or so down at the end of our road that had this service. I decided it was better to help a neighbor than to go somewhere else for this service, so I gathered up the knives and went to visit this neighbor.

He was working in his garage when I arrived and I cheerfully said "Hello", and introduced myself. I told him we were the people who had bought the farm just down the road from him. He nodded his head and in an indifferent tone he said, "Yep, I know." A pause.... Then he went on to say, "City folk!"

Well, I knew right then and there I wasn't welcomed, so I never returned to see this neighbor again. I left his shop wondering if I should I refer to him as well as other people in the area as "'Country folk?" I think not.

When we got situated after moving into our new residence, I was invited to join a group of women who got together once a month. They were all wives of the local families that owned and farmed the properties in the area. I felt this was a good way to meet and learn about my neighbors.

Once I joined this group, I found it quite interesting and sometimes humorous. There was one neighbor that seemed to be a little more sophisticated than the other neighbors in the group. At one meeting, she suggested that the next time we meet; she would like whoever was responsible for refreshments to make decent size cookies and not those *huge* farm size cookies!

In this group, it was expected at each meeting that someone would be nominated or should volunteer to give a presentation after they went to a class at the local county's Cooperative Extension Bureau. I never knew the Cooperative Extension Bureau to give classes on *anything*. I just thought they were there to answer any questions one may have regarding household affairs.

When it was my turn to give a presentation, I was to go to this Cooperative Extension class prior to the meeting and learn what they were teaching at that time. When I arrived there, I discovered the topic was on nutrition. As a result of the meeting, it turned out I learned for the first time that beans and rice prepared together make a complete protein! Who knew!?? Remember, that was over forty years ago and our country wasn't as conscientious about nutrition as we are now.

Chapter 6

The Parish Priest

and His Secretary

Once we moved into the farmhouse, I went to the local parish to register our family and meet the parish priest, as I was raised Catholic. When I walked in, I met the church secretary. Before she asked the purpose of my visit, she started to tell me all about her life. She said her name was Millie, but she said I could call her "Big M". She went on to say that she was a stripper before she came to town to become the priest's secretary. She told me she and the priest were neighbors and grew up together in Pittsburgh. This was quite a fascinating conversation to say the least.

Once I was registered, I had no clue that the priest would one day stop by the house for a visit.

One afternoon there was a knock on the door. When I opened it, there stood our parish priest! He said he was stopping by to bless the house. I was quite surprised to see him since I never experienced a priest to do this before, so I invited him in. As fate would have it, my sister, her husband, and their four children were visiting us at the time.

The priest started to walk through the house sprinkling holy water here and there. The house was designed so you could walk all around the first floor continuously in a circle through the rooms.

I followed him and to my shock as he was passing our bathroom, I saw my sister sitting on the commode with the door wide open! I hastily closed the door as we walked by and to this day, I don't know if the priest saw her or not. He never said a word and I didn't either.

The pastor held annual bazaars to help support the church. The following year I went to my first bazaar. When I arrived that afternoon, a bunch of people were sitting in chairs playing music on top of the flat bed of a semi truck in the church's parking lot. However, the music was no ordinary music; it was a Kazoo band!

I was there less than an hour when "Big M" came out of the rectory with a white bra on over her T-shirt with two tassels hanging on the bra.   She performed with the Kazoo band by making these tassels on her bra do their 'thing" while she bumped and grinded. The priest was nowhere to be seen. I don't know if he knew she was doing this or not. If he knew about it, I'm sure he didn't want to show his face under the circumstances. After being there a while, I left to drive back home, just smiling to myself and shaking my head.

Chapter 7
A Slight Culture Shock

At that time of my life I had quite a sweet tooth. I was young and skinny and could get away with eating sweets so I was always happy to see a bakery. One ritual I used to love was to go to a local bakery after Sunday Mass and enjoy a breakfast of some fresh baked pastries when I got back home. I soon found the village's only bakery and was happy to think I could continue my Sunday ritual.

When I visited the bakery one day, I noticed they had a lemon meringue pie. Mark, as well as myself, really liked a good fresh lemon meringue pie, so I kept this bit of information tucked in my memory bank.

One day I had nothing sweet in the house so I went to the bakery to get that lemon meringue pie. When I arrived, I didn't see any pies in the case and I asked the lady about it. She very slowly and sweetly told me that they only baked two lemon meringue pies on Tuesday morning, and if I got there very early that day, I would be able to get one. Oh groan!

Chapter 8
Make Hay While the Sun Shines

As I mentioned previously, our farming neighbors rented a good portion of our land to plant their crops. However, I was surprised to learn after we moved in that summer, that we had inherited a field of hay in back of the house. The neighbor said they would cut and bale the hay for us but it was up to us to load it on our truck and store it in the barn.

The weather was great when the hay was cut and baled, but the forecast was for rain in the very near future. I was told we had to get the bales of hay in the barn before the bales got wet so they wouldn't mold. Moldy hay and animals don't mix.

Mark had bought a very old Chevy truck to have around for farm projects. I don't remember the year of the truck, but it was old enough that the ignition starter was in the floor of the truck.

Mark and the two older girls hurried to load the back of the truck with the bales of hay and it was my job to start and stop the truck, as it constantly stalled while it was idling. I had to practically stand to reach the truck's starter on the floor because I had to have the truck's seat far enough away from the steering wheel to make room for the protrusion of the oncoming event. Besides that, I had to have room to shift gears as well because the gearshift was *also* on the floor.

To everyone's great relief, the bales of hay were all collected, removed from the truck and stacked securely in the barn. All was accomplished before the rains came the next day.

Farm Lesson 1: Make hay while the sun shines.

Chapter 9
Farm Lesson #2

We are now going to the large entrance room with the corner fireplace. We never had a fireplace before and knew nothing about the importance of keeping the flu vent closed. (Actually, I discovered later there wasn't even a flu vent to close!) Mark had to make something to fit up in the chimney to close the large opening.

One early October evening, Mark needed to go to town for something. While he was gone, I heard a scream from one of the girls. When I got to the TV room where they were sitting, I realized what the commotion was all about; there was a bat flying around the room! The bat had come down through the chimney and flew out from the open fireplace into the rooms.

I told Charlotte to go up the back stairs to one of the bedrooms so she wouldn't see the bat and be afraid of what was going on. I got a broom and kept swinging at the bat to try to get it out of the house. Needless to say, with the built-in radar that bats have, I was quite unsuccessful!

Finally Mark pulled in the drive. I met him at the door with broom in hand. When he got in the house, he tried to swing at the bat with the broom as I did. Mark, too, realized in a very short time that the bat was winning. He managed to maneuver the bat back into the TV room and closed both doors to the room. He then went to get his pistol and before I knew it, four shots were fired into the family room's woodwork and the bat was on its way to bat heaven!

The bullet holes were still in the woodwork right up to the day we sold and left the house. I actually forgot all about that until I wrote this chapter! Lesson to be learned, never leave the fireplace flu open when there's no fire in the fireplace!

Chapter 10
Terri's Tribulations

Before we moved to the farm, our oldest daughter Terri was having dizzy spells. One time when I took her and her sister Marie to the doctor's office to be examined for a cold and a possible ear infection, Terri passed out and hit her head on the examining table! This stunned both the doctor and me.

She came to after getting a whiff of the smelling salts the doctor waved under her nose. After I told him she had been having some dizzy spells lately, he felt she needed to be examined further by a neurologist. I told him we were in the process of moving to the southern part of the state, and he suggested that I go to either Buffalo or Rochester to see a neurologist. I felt there was no difference in distance between the two locations so I decided to see a neurologist in Rochester, since I knew the area there better than I knew Buffalo.

After Terri went through a series of tests at a well renowned hospital, we were informed that they were afraid her dizzy spells were caused from a growth at the base of her head that may not be operable. I was numb when I heard this news. I guess I was so numb that the doctor's secretary told me some time after our baby was born that they couldn't get over my composure when I was told the news.

The neurologist suggested we have a second opinion, which we did. The second doctor said what he saw on the tests were nothing to be concerned about. We were elated to hear this news! My daughter was delighted and relieved as we were! She confided in us later she was afraid an earlier planned family vacation would be canceled because of her.

The Neurologist felt Terri's dizzy spells were petite mal seizures and prescribed medication for this. After taking this for a while, Terri complained that she felt the medication made her thinking seem foggy and her senses feel numb or dull.

When Terri and I communicated this to the doctors, (we saw several different neurologists over the years), they all said that this medication didn't have that kind of side affect. Terri insisted that she continued to feel this discomfort and wasn't happy about how it made her feel. However, she was at the age where she wanted to learn to drive and if she was ever going to drive, she had to be seizure free for a couple years, so she agreed to continue to take the medicine.

One late summer day, I looked out the kitchen window and saw Terri lying on the road. It looked as though she had fallen from her bicycle and I ran down the road to her. Before I could get to her, our next-door neighbor was driving down the road at the same time, and he stopped to help her.

The neighbor knew I was pregnant and didn't want me to see her in the bloody condition she was in and insisted I not go near her. Of course I ignored his advice and yelled to call an ambulance. It was obvious she was in the midst of what I thought was a grand mal seizure.

While in the ambulance, my daughter continued to go in and out of what seemed to be separate seizures during the ten-mile ride to the hospital. She continued to do this for a good length of time in the hospital also. We later learned she was having what the neurologist described as a "status" epileptic seizure.

We learned several years later the difference between a status seizure and a grand mal seizure is that when a person experiences a status seizure, instead of a doctor walking to the patient, the doctor *runs* to the patient! I guess ignorance can be bliss at times, especially when I was then eight months pregnant. The doctors and neurologists seemed to be quite hushed about it at the time.

Later, Terri confessed to me that prior to her fall from the bike, she had quit taking her medication for about two weeks. She reminded me how dull she felt her thinking became and no one believed her. She went on to tell me that the two weeks she was off the medication, for the first time in a long time she could think so much clearer.

However, sadly for her, she still needed to continue to take the medication to prevent the seizures. Years later when we saw a different neurologist, Terri mentioned to him how she felt while taking the medication and how the other doctors denied that this was true. We both breathed a sigh of relief when he said, "Yes, I know how it makes you feel, because I tried taking it myself, and it *can* dull your senses and thinking!"

Chapter 11
The Pending Period

We are now getting closer and closer to welcoming our surprise event. In spite of the energy I had expended during the move to the farm, I seemed to gain more weight than usual with this pregnancy. The doctor suggested I start to visit him more frequently, especially since we lived so far away. This way, he said we could have a better idea when to anticipate the baby's birth.

Now I had to make the three-hour round trip drive to see the obstetrician every two weeks. (Since then, new expressways have been constructed and it isn't that long a drive.) I was getting huge and growing out of my maternity clothes.

One week when I visited the doctor I was just CERTAIN he would take me in that day to have the baby and I wouldn't have to make the trip back to the farm. I even packed a small suitcase to take with me just in case! Instead, the doctor said I was in no way near the time due for delivery. My heart sunk. I told him, "At that rate, by the time I come here for the next visit, I will need to be wheeled in here in a wheelbarrow!"

Then one morning at 2:00 a.m., I got an unexpected nudge from the "expected", and we were headed north for the hospital! Marie, our middle daughter called out to me from her bedroom as we were leaving the house and said, "Bring back a boy, Mom!" I told her not to put so much pressure on me. My only sister just had her 4th daughter five weeks before this baby was to be delivered and as you know, we already had three daughters, so we just didn't feel it was possible.

When our next door neighbor knew the time was getting close to the delivery time, she was gracious enough to offer to watch the girls if we needed her. We took her up on this offer and we were truly grateful to have her.

The drive to the hospital was an hour and a half away and Mark managed to drive it in 45 minutes! Some grueling time later, an 8 lb. 8 oz. baby boy with hands and feet the size of lion's paws, was born! He was named Thomas and he was born the third week in October.

This neighbor was watching our youngest, five-year-old Charlotte, when her sisters came home from school the day their brother was born.

Our middle daughter Marie asked our neighbor if she had a brother or sister. When our neighbor told her she had a baby brother, Marie started to cry.

Charlotte looked at her quite puzzled and couldn't understand why she was crying. Marie tried to explain to her sister that she wasn't crying because she was sad or upset, but because she was happy! Our neighbor told us that every time Marie tried to explain this to Charlotte, Marie couldn't get the words out because she was crying so much.

Mark then called my Mom and Dad to tell them the news. They quickly drove the four and a half hours to our farm to help watch the children and to help me when I arrived home.

The day after I was home from the hospital, Mark came in the house with a bushel of apples he had purchased along the roadside on his way home from work. He gleefully said he thought it would make great applesauce for us to can. My heart sunk but Mom and I couldn't let the apples spoil so we pared, cored, sliced and cooked a lot of applesauce the next day.

When Mark came home from work the next day, he asked if the apples made good applesauce. I answered him truthfully that they were great apples and cooked up especially well.

He said, "Great! Tomorrow I'll get another bushel for you!" I stood there in shock with my gut twisting and before I could say anything, my mother yelled, "No, you won't!"

Mark looked at her in astonishment for talking to him like that. I was so relieved she said that because I didn't have the nerve or the energy to tell him "no". Not another bushel of apples arrived at our household that fall!

Chapter 12

Wanton Winds

Since Mark is a hunter and hunting season starts in November, he drove to northern Pennsylvania to go hunting that first year. While he was gone, a brutal windstorm came up one evening. It was the first windstorm I had experienced on the farm. The wind blew so strongly through the night that I truly feared the house was going to cave in. The walls and windows creaked so that I thought the windows might fall out of their frames or the glass in the windows might shatter.

Our bedroom was in the southwest part of the second floor and that was the direction the wind was blowing from. The baby was only a month or so old, so he was still sleeping in our bedroom. Because of the intense winds, I feared for his safety so I took him downstairs to a safer area in the house and stayed there the rest of the night.

The next day I learned the windstorm had blown all the Christmas lights and decorations off from the front of a large department store in downtown Rochester!

We had many windstorms in those four years while living on the farm. One windstorm was so bad that the wall *in the center* of our home shook so hard that the large framed picture hanging on that wall shook as though it was possessed.

That particular day, the girls were in school. I paced back and forth in the house wondering how they were going to get home from school on the bus. I was relieved when the schools sent the children home early because of the high winds. It was the first I ever knew a school to send children home because of high winds that weren't tornado or hurricane winds!

Another time another windstorm blew so furiously outside that when I woke the next morning, I noticed from my bedroom window there were a lot of holes in the walls of the barns! After the storm we went to investigate and discovered the holes were actually *doors* we never knew existed in the barns and the wind blew them all off their hinges! All of the doors! All off!!

The barn also had a large overhang on the north side. After each windstorm the overhang had to be replaced because it would never stay on and it was constantly being blown off.

Chapter 13
A Slight Catastrophe

It was early February and our baby was now three months old. Mark came home one evening and announced that he invited an executive from work with his wife and family for dinner over the weekend. Being the Debbie Domestic I wanted to be, I decided to bake cookies and make bread dough from scratch for dinner rolls for dinner. My two older daughters and I were baking the cookies while the bread dough was rising while I was preparing the dinner. Everything was under control.

The ground was still snow covered and Mark, wearing his snowmobile outfit, was outside cutting wood with his chainsaw so we could have a fire in the fireplace while the friends were here. Then out of nowhere I heard Mark shout, "**PEG**"! My heart stopped. I knew something was awry.

I went to the back porch and there was Mark sitting on the floor, holding his leg together through the tear in the snowmobile outfit with blood streaming everywhere! He yelled to get a bottle of antiseptic. When I gave it to him he just poured the contents of the bottle into the wound.

My oldest daughter tried to call the ambulance but got very emotional in the stress of the moment. I took the phone and told the ambulance station that it was the old Chapman farm on Ireland Road. We waited and waited for the ambulance to arrive. Finally I felt we couldn't wait any longer so I drove Mark to the hospital. As I was driving, we passed the ambulance on the way to our place. I stopped them to tell them I couldn't wait any longer and I was taking him to the hospital myself. I discovered later, the ambulance driver went to the Ireland farm on Chapman Road and that was why they were so late in arriving at our place!

When we got to the hospital and I saw the size of the hole in Mark's leg, I felt there was no way they could possibly close the wound without having to graph some extra skin or something to the wound. It looked as though a wild animal had taken a chunk out of it! However, what do I know?!? Surprisingly, they were able to close the wound with several stitches and we were on our way back home.

When I arrived at the house, the same neighbor that watched the girls when our son was born was again very gracious to come over and keep an eye on things. Together, the girls and our neighbor finished baking the cookies but the bread dough was a sight! By that time, the bread dough had risen to the point where it was *literally* hanging over the counter and was half way down the front of the cabinets!

Our neighbor told me later that when she saw me walk in the kitchen that afternoon after bringing Mark back from the hospital, she thought I looked as though I had been pulled through a knothole. Thanks neighbor, for that unique description!

By this time, as I'm observing Mark walking around the house in pain while needing the assistance of a cane, I figured the only reasonable thing to do was to cancel the dinner. *WRONG!* After we came back from the hospital, Mark's friend called to confirm the time of dinner. Mark told them what had occurred. His friend said he was very sorry to hear that and they would come another time. Mark said, "No, no, no! Come on down. Everything is fine!" I could have strangled him*!*

After we had dinner, our guest's wife noticed a basket in the corner of the dining room. She was quite surprised to find a baby in the basket (which was actually a bassinet.) Our three month old son had slept very quietly through all of the commotion and *again*, I was grateful!

Chapter 14

The Mischievous Master

Since my parents had never allowed me to babysit, I didn't know anything about taking care of babies. After having three daughters over a period of eleven years, I had finally gotten the hang of taking care of female babies. However, now I'm faced with a completely different set of circumstances; a boy baby! Once we came home from the hospital, the first thing that needed to be attended to was that our little son had to have his diaper changed.

Yes, I still changed those things called diapers. We couldn't have Pampers because Mark had developed an allergy to them when I first used them for our youngest daughter Charlotte, so I had to continue to use cotton diapers.

Well, once I removed his diaper, there was this extra scab that needed to be taken care of besides the one for his navel! Then after recovering from that shock, was the shock of trying to stop that little hose of his from spraying all over the ceiling and wallpaper! It took a few diaper changes before I finally got the knack of resolving that dilemma. However, I noticed when I first took Tommy to the pediatrician and the pediatrician opened his diaper, he too, still wasn't used to the spraying! After observing this, I didn't feel too badly when I discovered others seemed to have the same problem when they offered to help by changing his diaper!

As the months flew by, Tommy began to walk, which got him into some innocent shenanigans. He never napped and was never tired even at midnight. I know if I had him first, we probably wouldn't have had three other children!

Just because he wasn't tired, didn't mean his mother wasn't tired. I would put him to bed in his crib for a nap or to sleep at night, and he would constantly crawl out of the crib.

One night I decided to lie on the floor beside his crib and monitor him until he fell asleep. (There was no such thing as a baby monitor at that time.) When all seemed to be quiet in his bedroom while I was still lying on the floor, I checked his crib to see if he really was asleep. My heart stopped! He wasn't in his crib! I couldn't figure where he could possibly be because I was lying on the floor right next to the doorway so he couldn't get passed me if he did get out of the crib and I knew I didn't fall asleep!

I finally found him up against the wall between the crib and the wall with two big eyes looking right at me. Somehow, he had climbed out of the crib in-between the crib's railing and the wall. He was as silent as could be and was just waiting for the right time to continue to move on.

I was beside myself. I had no idea what else to do to get him to stay in his bed and to get him to sleep! Eventually, he grew out of that phase and stayed in his crib. However, it was quite exhausting for me until that time arrived. His sisters really spoiled me when they took three-hour naps in the afternoon and in the evening went to bed *early* and *stayed there*!

On one occasion when company was visiting us and we were all sitting around the table in the kitchen, Mark decided to go out to the barn with his friend. He went to put his boots on but once he got his one foot in the boot, he left out a yell! Everyone turned quickly to see what he was yelling about.

Mark slowly took his foot out of the boot and there was this oozy, gooey stuff dripping from his sock. Somehow, without anyone seeing or knowing about it, our son had gotten a fresh egg from the refrigerator and put it in his father's boot. He was just a little over a year old at the time, but he was already starting to learn how to play pranks on people.

There was another time when I decided I needed to clean the woodwork on the first floor. There was a hallway area between the kitchen and the TV room and I decided that was the woodwork that needed to be cleaned. I was scrubbing away on my hands and knees and when I got to the end of the hall, I stood up to look back to admire the results of my hard work. I gasped when I discovered that unknown to me, our very young son was right behind me all the time, and very quietly was on his hands and knees with a red crayon in hand, drawing on all the woodwork I had just freshly cleaned!

Our son was about a year and a half old and still wasn't talking. One day Tommy decided to draw a mural with crayons all over the whole length of the back of the wallpapered wall in our TV room. He then searched for me and proudly showed me what he had done. Not wanting to deter this creative ability, I didn't scold him for doing this since we had planned to replace the paper in that room soon. I did tell him in so many words that it was not an appropriate medium for him to use.

However, our son was so proud of his masterpiece mural (a mural I planned to keep from inquisitive visitor's eyes by quickly ushering them into the living room until we repapered), that one day he quickly took the first visitor that arrived by the hand and directed them into the TV room. He then stood there in a very proud stance, one hand on one hip and the other hand moving from left to right to display his masterpiece mural.

Although he wasn't very old at the time, he was already showing his artistic talents. Many years later this talent won him honors and awards in high school and college. One year he was even awarded his own private art studio in college! He also received a medal for his artwork at his college graduation, which was only one of the many medals he received that day.

One afternoon I discovered a beautiful iridescent green bug on the dining room floor. I decided this would be a good opportunity to teach Tommy an early biology lesson. I called him into the room and showed him the colorful bug. I went on to exclaim how beautiful it was and I elaborated on the size and shape of the bug, etc. He stood there for a moment taking in all that I said, and then in a flash ---

--- he stomped on the bug and killed it!   End of lesson!

A few months later there was an incident with our son that could have proven to be much worse than it was.   As I mentioned earlier in the book, our driveway circled around our house like a crescent and the far side of the crescent was on an incline. The flat part of the driveway was at the top of the circle, and faced the back door of the house. We always entered and left the house through the back door and parked our cars there where it was flat. On the far side of the slanted part of the driveway was a deep ditch that allowed the flow of water to pass during rainstorms.

One day I had just driven back to the house after getting groceries and had parked the bus at the top of the driveway in front of the back door to unload. At the time, we had a VW bus, which we felt was practical for us to have with the four children.

I took our son from the bus and let him go to run and play while I removed the groceries. While I was putting the groceries away in the house, one of the girls came into the kitchen yelling that their brother was in the bus in the ditch!

I tore out of the house with Mark right behind me scolding me for leaving the keys in the car. I yelled back that I did no such thing! When I got to the bus in the ditch, there was our son standing on the front seat looking back at us fearfully screaming his lungs out!

At that time in the 70's, the emergency break in the VW bus was on the floor and stood up in the air like a stick with indented marks on it for your fingers. I don't know if that design has ever changed.

When I opened the car door, Tommy pointed to the emergency break and sobbingly told me, "I pulled the gun! I pulled the gun!" Good glory! How on earth could that child have reached that high to reach the car door's handle to open the bus' door to get it open!? How did he even step up that high into the bus to get in, as I always had to carry him in and out of it! Well, one more lesson learned; never underestimate a little boy's curiosity!

One evening when Mark and Tom were having a little bonding time and Tommy was sitting on his Dad's lap, Mark noticed a lump on the side of Tom's neck. He became even more alarmed when he noticed a couple more small bumps. We panicked. Mark, working in the pharmaceutical industry, had some knowledge of medicine and he immediately thought it might be Hodgkin's Lymphoma.

The next day I made an appointment with the pediatrician in the village. After she checked Tom all over, she suggested I take him to see a pediatrician surgeon in Rochester. I immediately made the appointment. Once the surgeon saw the bumps in Tom's neck, he asked me, "Had this young boy ever been scratched by a cat on this side of his head?" The surgeon pointed to a specific place on Tom's head.

I said, "Yes, he was!"

I told him that Tommy had gotten in-between two cats fighting in the back yard and one cat scratched him in that area of the head. I had called our pediatrician in the village and he said to clean the scratch and put disinfectant on it. He then went on to tell me to call him if I felt I noticed any changes in Tom, which I never did.

The pediatrician surgeon then told me that Tommy had "Cat Scratch Disease". I had never heard of any such thing! The surgeon asked me to see him periodically so he could continue to check Tommy to see if the lumps grew in size and to decide what to do if they did. All of us were relieved to learn it wasn't Hodgkin's disease, but it was still quite a concern for us.

As Tommy got older his sisters continued to give him gifts and I realized this young man was not learning the social graces of sharing. I was constantly scolding the girls for giving him so much and for doing everything for him. It was a mixed blessing for both Tommy and I; I was happy the girls weren't being selfish with the newer addition to the family, but I also knew that this young boy had no way to give back to them and for that reason, he was only learning how to 'take'. The girls would do all kinds of things for him and I would tell them he had to learn to do things for himself but it seemed to go in one ear and out again.

Since we lived away from any children that were even close to his age, I decided it was time to find a place where there were other children to play with and for him to learn the fine art of sharing. The small town we lived in at the time had no preschool, so I checked around to find some kind of reliable day care service. Someone referred me to a very reliable home for this kind of service in the village.

I took Tommy there one day with the hope he would learn that the world didn't revolve around him. When I picked him up at the end of the day, I was curious to discover if he benefited at all from this new kind of social activity. The woman said that Tommy had a few moments of puzzlement when he discovered all the toys weren't his. She said as the day progressed, he kind of figured it out. I took him there once a week until we learned we needed to move to another state. I have no idea how his personality would have developed if he hadn't received this service.

Chapter 15

Our Edifying Animals

When we had been on the farm a month or so, Mark felt we needed to have some animals, so he decided to get several cows, some calves, a horse, and raise a litter of dogs. A friend of ours knew someone who had a quarter horse, which we purchased and named Melissa. The only reason we didn't raise chickens, was because a neighbor down the road from us had chickens and sold eggs, so we didn't want to compete with them.

While attempting to raise animals on the farm, I found it quite interesting to discover that animals aren't as ignorant as we humans would like to think they are. Like children who choose to be mischievous or need your attention the moment you are on the phone, our cows and the horse would choose a time when Mark was out of town to find a way to leave the barnyard and roam the countryside! How they knew this, I have no clue!

For example, Terri and Marie raised and trained two of the cows we had for 4-H. The girls worked really hard and followed all the instructions the 4-H leader taught them. They had to learn how to break the cows from being somewhat wild and untrained, to being able to lead them in a docile manner around the ring at the County Fair. However, the cows liked their independence more than they liked being led around a ring and they were always finding ways to leave the barnyard. When this happened, we would have to scurry after them as they ran across the fields and through the neighbor's yards. This mainly occurred when Mark was on a business trip or worked late at the office -- the office that was an hour away. Then the two older girls and I would need to call all the neighbors in the near-by area and ask them if they saw our cows and/or horse, to please contact us so we would know what direction to go to look for them. Then we would scour the neighborhood trying to find our adventurous animals. When this happened at night, my main concern was that the cows might wander onto the highway that was not too far from our home. If a car hit either a cow or the horse, someone could get seriously hurt.

During these episodes, I came to learn that when a cow runs away, you *never* run after them! If possible, you find a way to get in front of them with a pail of grain and generally they will follow you back to the barnyard just to get the food. Mark tried to overcome these episodes of runaway cows by fixing the barnyard gate so the cows wouldn't have a chance to get out. It seemed they were able to pull the gate latch directly across with their teeth for the gate to open, wait until the gate fell back against the fence, and then they would walk to freedom. When we finally realized that type of latch wasn't working, Mark nailed several stacks of wood on top of each other on the gate latch so it would be high enough to keep the cows from sliding the latch back with their teeth. Since the latch was now obstructed with these stacks of wood, for us to get in and out of the barnyard, we had to lift the latch up high enough to go over the stack of wood to open the gate. We all felt satisfied this was the perfect solution to keep the animals from getting out of the barnyard.

However, one sunny summer afternoon after Mark had fixed the latch, I was resting on a recliner outside when I happened to look over towards the barnyard and saw one of the cows lifting the latch up over the stack of nailed wood with its teeth! The cow backed up and waited for the gate to swing open towards her, and walked out of the barnyard while I sat there frozen in amazement! This time Mark was home and when I yelled, he came out of the house and immediately started to run after the cow while the cow tore across the fields.

I yelled at Mark, "You don't run *after* the cow. He'll just run faster!" Of course, Mark didn't think I knew what I was talking about and kept running after the cow. I ran back to the barn and got a pail of grain and was able to run in front of the cow to lure her back into the barnyard.

Plan A and Plan B for keeping the animals secure in the barnyard were now obsolete. I don't remember what Plan C was, but whatever it was; we didn't have trouble with the animals leaving the barnyard after that.

We had one Holstein cow and two cows that were a cross between a Charolais and a Holstein. Charolais cows were beef cows raised originally in France. We tried to raise other cows but they seemed to be susceptible to getting the Scours. They contracted diarrhea, which can be fatal because of dehydration. The veterinarian would prescribe a huge pill the size of a small egg. The challenge was to get the pill far enough down the calves mouth and throat so they could swallow it. Mark would do this as long as he was home, but when he wasn't around, it was up to me to find a way to approach the situation.

The first time I tried to do this one morning, I figured the only way was to have one of my daughters hold the pill to place it in the calf's throat while I straddled the calf and backed the calf into a corner of the barn. This way I could open the calf's mouth without the calf running away. While I held its mouth open, my daughter would drop the pill down his throat and then we massaged the calves' throat so the pill would go down instead of back up out of the calf's mouth. After doing this religiously for days, the calf still died. It was sad for all of us. You can get quite attached to the animals.

We had a full size Holstein with Scours one time. The veterinarian had the cow stay overnight a couple nights at their hospital, but we still lost the cow. After that we didn't buy any more cows. We just kept the ones the girls had for 4-H and a black and white Hereford named Blackie.

The two older girls had to get up very early every morning before school to make sure the cows were fed and had water before they went to school. They repeated the same routine when they got home from school every afternoon. This meant they had to wear separate overalls every morning and every afternoon when they fed the animals so they wouldn't smell profusely of manure. These overalls had to be washed and dried twice a day to keep the odor from carrying us all away!

Then there was the mud that was tracked in on the kitchen floor every day that needed to be cleaned, as I didn't want unsuspected visitors arriving and thinking I never kept a clean house. I felt I had to do this because I could generally rely on Mark to invite someone to dinner without telling me ahead of time.

For example: I had a stove with two ovens and I loved it! One day I decided it was time to clean both ovens. There were no self-cleaning ovens then, so the task took quite some time to do. I had just finished cleaning them in time to cook dinner before Mark came home from work. However Mark arrived home with a salesperson that was visiting the company in Rochester that day and he had not mentioned this.

I apologized to the salesperson about the condition of the home because I had been cleaning the double ovens all day. Tommy was three years old at the time and he supported my conversation with the guest by saying, "Yah. See?" And he proudly opened both oven doors for the salesperson to inspect as if he had cleaned the ovens himself!

Back to the animals: One day Mark was fixing the stalls in the barn while Blackie, our black and white Hereford was there with him. Mark was bending over while hammering away at one of the stalls. Blackie then decided it was an opportune time to go over to Mark, see what was going on, and then tried to mount him. Surprised, Mark turned around and in self-defense, hit the cow on the head with the hammer he was using to fix the stalls.

I was told that Blackie just stepped back, shook his head, looked a little dazed, and went back to try to mount Mark again and again. Mark repeated his self-defense tactics to no avail until he was finally able to get to his feet and get out from Blackie's aim of fire. Blackie had been 'fixed' sometime before this incident occurred but I guess it didn't fix Blackie's memory. After that we referred to Blackie as the "queer steer".

We had a large field south of the barnyard where we would leave the horse to feed on the fresh grass and to exercise. We always had a large tub of water in the barnyard so the animals could drink whenever they were thirsty.

One day I planned to go to town to get some groceries and run some errands that morning. It had rained the night before and it was a cool and overcast morning, so I thought while I was gone it would be a good time to let the horse roam in the field that was adjoined to the barnyard. The fence that was around the grazing field and around the barnyard was electric, so I didn't feel there would be a problem with the horse getting away.

However, I didn't anticipate the day to turn sunny and hot while I was gone. As I was driving back to the house after doing my errands, I looked up towards the barn and saw our horse Melissa frantically leaning against the gate to get into the barnyard to get some water. I jumped out of the car and ran to the gate to open it for her. She must have been either very desperately thirsty, or mad as hell with me for leaving her out there in the field, or both, because she slammed me up against the fence with the gate she was leaning against and rushed to the barnyard to get to the water.

Because of the rainstorm the night before, I was standing at the time in a pool of water up over my feet. The force of the gate threw me up against the electric fence pinning me there while I was standing in the water. The shock of the electricity went all through my body! I tried to let go of the fence, but it seemed like forever before I could shake my hands free from the electric barbwire. The sensation of feeling that electricity go through my body was an experience I didn't soon forget! I found myself understanding the kind of torture I heard about when they told of people having to stand in water while electric cattle rods were placed to their privates.

There was also the time when our horse Melissa accidently stepped on a nail and Mark called the veterinarian to come to the farm to remove it. Naturally, Mark had to go to work that day. When the veterinarian arrived, he had to anesthetize her in order for him to remove the nail. With the horse still standing on all four legs and with her being anesthetized, she kept leaning to one side. The veterinarian feared she would fall over so he asked me to lean against the opposite side of Melissa to prevent her from falling while he removed the nail. Well, that was like trying to prop up a ton of bricks! After a certain amount of perseverance on both the veterinarian's part and myself, the nail was removed from the horse's foot and all was well after Melissa had a good nap.

At the top of a hill on our farm, we had a ten-acre hickory nut grove, which made an ideal pasture for the cows to graze. I thought this pasture was beautiful. The pasture was high enough on the hill that you could overlook the Mount Morris Dam at Letchworth Park, which was about 4-5 miles away (as the crow flies). At one time I seriously looked for a spot in that hickory nut grove for me to be buried.

In the spring, Mark would take the three cows to the pasture up on the hill. He would bring them back to the barn every now and then and also before winter set in. On one occasion when he was in the process of bringing one cow back to the barnyard, the cow decided to take off running and she was not running in the direction of the barnyard! I guess the cow decided she liked the independence of being in the pasture compared to going back to the isolation of the barnyard. This caught Mark off guard and he slipped and fell. When he fell, the rope he was using to lead the cow, looped around his boot and got caught around his ankle. The cow dragged him across the wide-open spaces and no one knew how to stop her!

The girls came running to the house to tell me what was happening. By the time I got there, Mark was free. Mark was wearing cowboy boots at the time and he said that his boot eventually got pulled off from the rope. All of us were more than relieved because the cow was headed straight towards a pile of old telephone poles that were stacked up on the side of our property which was left by the utility company. Otherwise it could have been a far worse catastrophe than it actually was.

We also had a lot of cats on the farm; none of whom we purchased. They just came and went as their owners dropped them off along the roadside when they felt they could no longer keep them for whatever reason. I guess the cats' survival instincts set in because they managed to find our barns and helped us immensely by keeping control of unwanted rodents. There were some absolutely beautiful cats that found their way to our place. None of them had names; they just knew when to come when I set milk and food out for them.

We became more attached to some cats than others. There were times, sadly, when fate would intervene and we would lose a few. This was usually when a cat would find a nice warm car engine to crawl up inside to take a nap. Then when the driver of the car would start to leave and turn the car on, we would hear an ungodly screeching noise coming from under the hood. Alas, one more cat missing from duty.

Mark, being the avid hunter, loved to train hunting dogs. Because of his interest, he decided this was a good time to raise a litter of German Wirehaired Shorthairs with the help of our two oldest daughters.

The mother was bred right after Mark purchased her and soon she had her first litter of puppies. This was the mother's first litter of pups so the morning she began to deliver, she was quite frightened. That morning the girls were feeding the cows and horse and discovered the mother was in the process of delivering her puppies. The mother, not knowing or realizing what was happening to her, was lying on top of a couple of her puppies and the girls were afraid she might suffocate them. The girls wanted to stay by her side until all the puppies were born. I knew they couldn't do this and still go to school so I gave them *my* dispensation that they could stay home until all the puppies were born.

When the girls went to school the next day, I had written a note to their teachers regarding their reason for missing school and explained the ordeal that had occurred the previous day. A note came back from the girls' teachers telling me it was an illegal absence. I accepted that fact, but if need be, I would have done the same thing again.

This dog had the sweetest looking puppies. However, as the puppies grew older, we discovered there was one dog in the litter that, much to our dismay, was a cat killer! Every time this dog had a chance, he would tear after the cats and before we knew what was happening, he would kill them by grabbing them by the scruff of the neck and shook them until they died, one by one! For this reason we were very much on guard with this particular dog and made sure that whenever he was out of the pen that there would be no cats around. He became the reason we were now down to only one mother cat. We desperately tried to protect this cat from this cat-hating dog.

One afternoon, much to my horror, the cat was accidently left out of the house at the same time the "cat-hating dog" was out of the kennel. I yelled to one of the girls to get the cat back in the house, but before anyone could react, in one swift second the dog grabbed the cat and tore off to the field with it! I ran after the dog and tried to knock the cat loose from the dog's grip by hitting him over the head with a baseball bat. At that time I didn't care if I killed the dog or not! The dog acted as though he never felt a thing! He just kept the cat in his grip while I continued to scream and beat the dog on the head.

While I'm doing this, my twelve year old daughter Marie came out of the house and very calmly walked up to the dog, lifted the dog's tail and kicked him in the testicles! The dog instantly dropped the cat while I looked on in amazement! I had no clue as to where or how Marie knew what to do in a situation like that! It was obvious I certainly didn't know what to do! Maybe 4-H taught them more than I realized?

Then there was the time when I took the girls swimming. We lived a short distance from a large park and at the northern end of the park was an Olympic sized pool that all could use. In the summer when the girls were finished with their chores, I would take them and their friends to the park to go swimming.

One day on our way back home from the park, I had to stop and wait for a gaggle of geese to cross the road. Another one of my edifying discoveries: I discovered that day that geese are also quite stubborn and they too, have a way of getting their point across to you. These geese would not move! So I felt I had no choice but to get out of the car and try to chase the geese away from the road. Hah! Not on your life! They had an agenda of their own! All of the geese turned around and chased ME right back into the car! I had to sit there and wait patiently until they decided when *they* wanted to leave the road!

Chapter 16
The Inclement Seasons

As I mentioned earlier in the book, before we moved to Rochester and bought this farm, we lived our whole lives in a small town in western Pennsylvania. While living there, I only experienced one 20-inch snowfall during all of my thirty-four years. However, the first winter we lived in Rochester, the area had 144 inches of snow! That was a lot of shoveling!

The winters were brutal on the farm. Because our house sat high on a hill, the altitude caused the growing seasons to be a couple weeks later and shorter than the seasons in the lower surrounding areas.

One year I remember coming home from a meeting one evening during the first week in September, and to my dismay I discovered we were in the midst of a heavy frost! Our tomato plants had just started to bear fruit a couple weeks before, so I scurried from the car and went directly to the garden and pulled up all the tomato plants I could muster and put them inside the house. Why did I do this? I was told that if you wrap green tomatoes in newspaper, in time, they will ripen and then you can use them as you would if you picked them from the garden. I was delighted to learn that this tidbit of information was true, as we enjoyed ripe tomatoes late that fall and winter.

If the cooler weather wasn't bad enough, the wind as I mentioned before, was also brutal. I felt so badly for the girls and their having the responsibility of keeping the horse and cows fed and watered twice a day, every day, no matter how cold the temperature was or how windy the day was. I remember wringing my hands at times when there were early mornings they had to go out into a blinding snowstorm to feed the animals.

One time in particular kept us all on edge. During the winter, in order to keep the water tank from freezing, Mark had a light bulb hanging over the container of water for added heat and that seemed to do the job. That is until one very cold and dark winter morning. When the girls went out to feed and give the animals their water, they discovered to their horror that during the night the light bulb went out and the water in the deep container had frozen solid! The cows didn't have the water they needed and we panicked.

At first no one knew what to do. It was obvious the water tank couldn't be thawed in time to have drinking water for the animals before the girls went to school, so Marie and Terri continued to haul buckets of water back and forth from the house to the barn in that weather. After that, Mark bought some kind of heating device to put in the water to keep the water from freezing so they would never have to experience that dilemma again.

One day while waiting my turn with one of the children at the doctor's office, I met a pharmaceutical salesman who was also waiting his turn to see the doctor. I didn't know if this man was from Rochester or Buffalo, but he commented on how it seemed as though whenever he came to this village, it always seemed as though he was driving into another world. He mentioned to me that in the winter he always experienced a drastic change in the weather as soon as he hit the top of this one particular hill just before he got to town. I knew exactly the hill he was referring to because when I was at one of the neighborhood meetings one evening, they were all reminiscing about some of their personal encounters on various winter evenings, and that particular hill was brought into the conversation more than once.

Their stories were quite amazing. Two of the neighbors lived at the top of this particular hill and they told that when there would be blizzards, in the middle of the night there would be knocks on their doors from people who were stranded in the storms. People would start to drive up this hill in decent weather, but by the time they approached the top of the hill, the weather changed so drastically that they were trapped in snowdrifts.

They also told of a time when a snowplow drove by to clear the highway and plowed right into a snow covered car with a woman in it and never knew the car was there! Luckily the woman survived!

One neighbor that lived at the bottom of this hill, said at times she would look out her window to see it clear outside, but couldn't see her next door neighbor's house at the middle of the hill because the snow falling there was like a huge wall between them.

I encountered a similar experience one time on that same hill. Mark was in the hospital in Rochester after having some surgery done. It was just a little more than a week before Christmas and the neighbor who lived at the top of this hill offered to watch our son while I was at the hospital with Mark.

The day was clear but as I was leaving the hospital, it started to snow. The further I drove towards home; the more the snow began to accumulate and it fell faster than usual. As I drove past different intersections along the way home, I witnessed cars that had spun out all over the roads and ditches because they weren't able to stop in time for the traffic lights or stop signs. Some cars weren't able to get started on the slippery roads once they had stopped and some cars weren't able to stop once they got started. I was getting more nervous by the minute by this situation. We just bought a new Toyota and never took the time to get snow tires put on, but it seemed to grab the road very well.

I just kept on driving the hour drive towards our home. With the grace of God, I was doing fine until I reached this same particular hill just before you get to our farm. There, three quarters of the way up the hill, was a jackknifed tractor-trailer. I refused to get myself all rattled about this. I figured I could just go up the hill far enough to be able to turn onto a country road that was on the left side of the hill and go to our house on a back road.

It seemed like it was a good idea at the time if that side road wasn't already *plowed closed*! Oh God, now what? I felt I had no choice but to continue driving up this hill and pass the jackknifed truck and hope no one was coming from the other direction. Success! I got through that and kept on driving until I pulled into the driveway of the neighbor's home where my son was staying. That's when I drove right into a snowdrift in their driveway and couldn't get back out! Lucky for me, the neighbor had a couple of very strong young sons who shoveled and pushed my car out of the snowdrift so I could drive home unscathed!

There would be times after a snowstorm where I would need to travel into town to go to the grocery store. Since we lived on a hill with no other buildings or trees around to act as wind barriers, the wind blew freely. For this reason, the snow didn't accumulate as much around our place as it did in town. Sometimes when I drove into town I would be in shock and awe to see snowdrifts so high they were over the home's porch roofs and some drifts were midway past their second floor!

There was an occasion one April when Mark and I had to go to a meeting in Florida. My mother and father came to the farm to stay with the children while we were gone. As I mentioned, it was April and we had warm weather before we left, so I felt there was no reason to be concerned about the family.

One morning a few days into the meeting, an employee came to see us at breakfast and announced there was quite a snowstorm in Rochester. He said all the businesses were closed, including the pharmaceutical company where Mark worked. I don't know if that business had EVER closed before because of bad weather!

Immediately I thought of the children, my parents, the farm animals, and the girls having to feed and water them and I panicked again! We called them at once and talked to the older girls. They said the storm was amazing and all the roads were closed.

I asked how deep the snow was and they said it all depended on where you stood. They said, "If you are standing by the barn, it is up to your chest, but if you are standing by the house, it is just over your feet." I asked if they had everything they needed? "Oh, we are just out of milk", they said. "Out of milk", I cried! "How is the baby going to go without milk"!? Panic, panic, panic! They said not to worry. They would borrow some from the neighbor if they needed to do so before the roads were plowed.

When we arrived back in Rochester, there was a LOT of snow for Mark to shovel at the airport parking lot before we could get in the car to drive home. Since the weather had been so nice at home before we left for Florida, he didn't wear a coat so he was pretty cold by the time he was done.

Our farmhouse was over a hundred years old. After living in the house a couple years, we realized we were using an unusual amount of heating oil during the winter. (And it seemed the winters lasted at least 10 months!) Mark decided to check the attic and when he did, he discovered there was NO insulation in the roof at all!

Our kitchen was on the west side of the house and this is usually the direction where the wind comes from. The kitchen sink is also on the west wall of the kitchen with a non-insulated window over the sink. I'm sure nothing else was insulated in the house, because the kitchen floor was so cold. I finally had to resign to wearing the insulation that's inside snowmobile boots OVER my shoes when I worked in the kitchen during the winter! It was the only way I could keep my feet somewhat warm. That's when I fully realized the reason for that old potbelly stove that used to be in the kitchen when we first moved in!

That also happened to be the year when Nixon was president and he was having everyone ration Christmas lights and electricity in general, and our fuel oil doubled in price. We started getting concerned about how we were going to heat this huge old place. Mark had a contractor give us an estimate for insulating the roof. After getting the estimate, we decided we had no choice but to go ahead and have it done.

After this project was accomplished and we got the first couple heating bills, it was astonishing to discover how much the new insulation helped us. We saved more than half of the original cost of our heating bills! And that was with the walls still not being insulated and still having the old windows that were installed when the house was first built!

Chapter 17

The Unfair County Fair

The year after we moved to the farm, the two older girls joined the 4-H Club with their cows. They listened to the 4-H leader's instructions regarding what to do and how to care for their animals, especially if they planned to show them at the Fair in the late summer. They followed his instructions religiously. One of the requirements was to break a cow in so you could lead the cow in the ring with a rope. Our middle daughter Marie was scared to death of her cow but eventually, with perseverance, she broke the cow in so she could lead it. However, it was not her favorite pastime!

Our oldest daughter Terri attacked this task like a duck to water. She loved everything about training her cow. When Fair time came, they and all the other children that were showing their cows had to wash them down every morning with Whisk. This to me was a cold and messy job, but the young boys and girls did this with no objections.

The County Fair was usually held the second week in August. The girls would get up at the crack of dawn to travel 20 minutes away to the fairgrounds to be with their cows and to do all the chores that were necessary to get their cows in shape to be shown.

I remember one August morning it was an extremely cold 28 degrees! I drove to the fairgrounds to give the girls their winter jackets to wear while they washed the cows down. Looking back now, that temperature is hard to imagine, but it was an unusually cold month that summer and I have to remind myself that this was also because of the higher elevation.

Show time came for the cows at the fair and the girls did extremely well! So well that Terri who just loved working with her cow, came in second place and Marie who was afraid of her cow, received the Grand Champion ribbon!! Wonders never cease!!

Mark and I were not only excited, but also astonished! However, the other local families that had entered their cows were not happy at all. Then we learned that the girls couldn't go on to compete at the New York State Fair because their cows were a crossbred between a Charolais and a Holstein. Only full bred cows were accepted at the State Fair.

The next year the girls entered their cows again. This time we became quite disillusioned with the whole judging aspect. In order for cows to keep their ideal weight and to be healthy, it's very important that they not have to stand all the time and that they need to lie down.

Well, the first day the girls took their cows to the fair that second year, they were astonished to find that "the powers that be" only allowed Terri's and Marie's cows enough room in their stalls for the cows to stand, with no room for them to lie down! All the other cows at the fair had *more* than enough room to lie down. It was quite evident that our cows were the only cows to have stalls with such small spaces. The unhealthy conditions the cows were in were so obvious that I couldn't help but wonder why the spectators at the fair didn't say something to the Director as it was so obvious!

I then learned another lesson: even farmers have their own set of politics. Mark felt we should still continue to participate and stay there to show our cows and not to be quitters. However, the cows lost so much weight over those few days that they looked quite emaciated and it was quite sad. I felt very badly for them being caught up in a situation like this. It was very disillusioning for us and we never entered another fair after that. It wasn't worth it after discovering how badly the other farmers felt towards us. The girls only did what the 4-H leader taught them to do and eventually they and their cows got punished for it.

It just occurred to me as I'm rereading this last paragraph why this incident may have occurred: our cows couldn't go to the State Fair the previous year because they were crossbred. If we had continued to go to the county fair with our cows and win, that would have prevented the 4-H members with their full bred cows from having the chance to win and then have the chance to go on to the State Fair! I can understand this now. However, I don't understand why the Director and/or the 4-H leader didn't just tell us that our crossbred cows couldn't enter the fair, instead of allowing them to suffer and possibly get ill by not allowing them the room to lie down!

Chapter 18
The Magical Gardens

Mark and I had been married a little over thirteen years when we bought the farm. It took me that long to fully realize how obsessive my husband could be. I mainly learned this as I watched him plant the vegetable garden across the driveway from the house. The soil in the garden was extremely rich from the hundred years of fertilizer that had been tilled in the garden and Mark was happy to take advantage of this.

When I was in elementary school, my father planted a large Victory Garden during World War II and I observed his talents in this area. Even Mark's mother loved to grow plants and vegetables for most of her life.

However, Mark and I had never planted a garden of our own before we bought the farm. The reason was mainly because our first and former home was in the middle of ten acres of woods that allowed very little sun for anything to grow.

Now that we had a farm, we purchased many seed catalogs and shopped in seed stores and nurseries for our garden. The first year of this endeavor proved to be very successful! We never grew or even ate zucchini before, so Mark planted a dozen or more zucchini plants. As anyone who has ever grown zucchini before knows, they grew like wildfire before we got the chance to pick them! We joked at the size of the vegetables and said we could use the zucchini for baseball bats if we needed to! It wasn't until much later when we saw the correct size of zucchinis in the grocery stores that we realized they are to be picked much, much sooner than we thought. Mark would pick these very proliferate vegetables every morning and take them to work to give to all his co-workers. At first they were happy and grateful. However, one day Mark came home and said that the employees were asking if we had anything else other than zucchini? Ungrateful employees!

I loved to eat raw green bell peppers so we planted them along with yellow frying peppers and hot peppers. As the pepper plants were starting to show their budding fruit, I watched them eagerly with bated breath waiting for the first sweet bell pepper to grow large enough to be picked and eaten.

Finally the day arrived and I snatched it quickly before anyone else saw it and took a large bite as if I was eating an apple! There was a moment of confusion and silence and then I ran furiously to the house for water! The bell pepper I ate turned out to be a large and *very hot*, green pepper!!

Coming from a very Anglo-Saxon family and upbringing, I discovered the longer we lived on the farm that I was quite ignorant of many types of vegetables. The extent of my knowledge in my early years were potatoes, more potatoes, green beans, corn, lima beans, butter beans, carrots, peas, beets, acorn squash and a little bit of cauliflower once in a while, and more potatoes. I never had broccoli until I visited Mark's parent's home for dinner on occasions!

Why I'm mentioning this is because while friends of ours were visiting us one spring day and viewing our garden, she noticed asparagus that had gone to seed along the side of one garden. She was excited to see that. I told her I didn't know anything about asparagus and didn't think I would like it. She exclaimed that I didn't know what I was missing and took me over to the asparagus patch and showed me what it looked like growing before it went to seed. She then told me how to cook it. Well once I cooked it, I was hooked. I would go out to the asparagus patch in the morning and stand over those little nubbins and watch them grow until they were the right size to pick!

Once we realized how successful growing all these fresh vegetables were, the next year we decided to get more adventurous and try new items. We thought it would be fun to try purple string beans, cabbage, cauliflower, eggplant and Brussels sprouts.

The following year, Mark got more adventurous and dug a THIRD garden and used it to primarily plant different varieties of winter squash that we never heard of before and he also planted different kinds of pumpkins. That garden was so successful that Mark decided it would be a good idea for the kids to sell pumpkins along the roadside at Halloween time. That was a big hit and the girls sold everything that season!

However, all these vegetables needed to be preserved in some way and I was the chosen one to figure how to achieve this. I canned until we ran out of canning jars. I would then beg and borrow jars from friends and family and when I exhausted them, I froze everything. The excess of vegetables was getting to me and I was finding myself feeling quite guilty about it. (At that time there were no food pantries in our area or anything similar to that for us to donate some of our excess produce.) I also became more and more astonished at how obsessive Mark was becoming with planting so much!

One year he decided to plant four-dozen tomato plants. The garden was so rich that at one point during the peak of the growing season, I picked a peck of tomatoes from just *two tomato plants* and there were forty-six other plants for me to continue to pick! Then there were the green and yellow beans. I picked all the beans until the plants had almost finished producing. Mark upon learning this, then felt that was a signal for him to continue to plant more rows of green and yellow beans!! And he did just that! Awgh!

However, the garden was a lifesaver at times. Because we had so many visitors from all over the country and since I seldom knew when any of them would arrive, it was great to have one of the girls go out to the garden and pick a cucumber, a bell pepper or a tomato, as we needed them. Without realizing it, I took this for granted until one afternoon when I was preparing a meal for a family from Ohio, I asked my daughter to go to the garden to pick a cucumber. The visiting family's oldest daughter exclaimed, "Wow! That's amazing to just go to the garden and pick a cucumber; just like that!!" It never occurred to me until that moment that it was pretty neat to be able to do this. It's amazing how quickly we can sometimes become oblivious to what we have.

Back to the pepper plants: Mark received a hot pepper relish recipe from his mother. He decided he wanted some of this in our pantry for a condiment, so one day he set out to make it himself. He hooked up the old-fashioned grinder to the table in the kitchen and started grinding onions and hot peppers. We were all sitting around the kitchen table while he was doing this. It didn't take long before we all had to leave the kitchen because the air was so potent with fumes from the hot peppers that we could hardly see from the tears running down our faces. However, Mark was determined and he continued until his project was completed.

Mark must have felt that having a farm meant there was no limit to what you could have, make, plant, etc. When he was growing up, his parents made apple butter from scratch in an old copper kettle and used a long handled old wooden stirrer or paddle with a hole in the center of the paddle to stir. They would stir the apple butter all day until the sauce was just the right consistency for canning. Mark decided in the fall that we should make this apple butter product that his parents used to make. Oh Gawd!

He asked his Dad if he could have the old iron caldron and long wooden paddle since his parents weren't making apple butter anymore. Mark felt this could be a project the whole family could partake in; you know, "togetherness". Once he decided we should do this, he scouted the countryside for apples. He came back with at least ten or more bushels of apples for us to make applesauce for the brew while he made the bag of seasonings to stir in the pot. He kept this recipe hidden from everyone.

To this day I don't know what the secret herbs and spices were, nor do I care. Mark was content to be outside all day stirring the caldron of cut apples while we were inside peeling, coring, cutting apples, and cleaning and boiling canning jars. Then he would proudly take the quart jars of apple butter to the office at Christmastime and give them to everyone as gifts.

CHAPTER 19
Auction Action &
Farmhouse Furnishings

Since the farmhouse had eleven rooms and we moved to this farmhouse from a small three bedroom ranch home, needless to say we didn't have enough furniture to fill all these rooms nor the money to buy all new furniture. Our former home didn't have a dining room but the farmhouse had one. This meant (along with many other items), we needed furniture for the dining room. The former owners had dining room furniture, as well as other furniture that we wanted to buy from them but they said we couldn't do this because they were committed to having an auction before the house was sold. Everything was to be auctioned off by the auctioneer at a scheduled date.

They suggested that we go to their auction and then bid on what we wanted.

Once we were informed of the auction date, we took another trip back to the farm. WOW, what intense excitement I experienced that day!! I had no idea an auction could get your adrenalin flowing like it did! I was anticipating that no one would want the furniture, but that was not the case. There was another family that decided they wanted the dining furniture and kept bidding against us! We had decided on a set price for the dining room set and if the other party still wanted it after that price was reached, they could have it. We would just have to find something else.

I was sad to realize the furniture that fit so perfectly in the dining room may not be ours because of the bidding war. It wouldn't even need to be moved from another location because it was *right there*. We lost the bid on the china closet which I would loved to have owned, but it was the dining table and chairs that we needed the most. So we continued to bid on the buffet, dining table, and chairs. Then much to our surprise, the other family quit bidding and the furniture was ours! However, we still didn't have a china closet.

Well, that new experience was unique for us and the result was that we got hooked on auctions! We had many more rooms to fill so we spent our evenings reading the local newspapers for auctions that would be held in the area. There was a college town nearby that had lovely homes and sometimes the residents would move and they would have an auction. Sometimes an antique store would go out-of-business and they would have an auction. Those were great opportunities for us! It got so that on weekends, Mark would go in one direction to an auction and I would go in another to find more treasures for our home and for very little money.

One afternoon I went to an auction at a very lovely home in this college town because I was still in pursuit of a china closet. The home had a large glass bookcase and it went for more money than I felt we should or could afford. However, I got caught up in the lovely items being auctioned at the home and stayed to watch purely out of curiosity.

After many items were sold, all the interested buyers walked into the living room and the auctioneer started to take bids on a lovely all wool, off-white carpet. It was lush and the pile was deep and velvety looking. I think it was about 12 feet wide by 24 feet long. I knew our living room was long but I wasn't sure of its dimensions.

The auctioneer tried to get a bid started and I waited to see where the bidding was going. He couldn't get it to start any higher than $30. So I bid $35. Another party bid $40. I bid $50 and figured that would be it, I wouldn't bid anymore, and I would head home. The auctioneer kept asking for another bid and no one would bid higher so the carpet was mine!

I was so thrilled that I went to the owner of the house and apologized for buying the carpet at such a reasonable price! Yah, I did that. I left figuring that if the carpet was too large for our living room, 'what the heck', we can always cut it and bind it on the one end.

When I got home and told Mark about my treasure, he was furious! I was shocked at his reaction. Couldn't he see how lovely this carpet was? Well, our beautiful collie dog also thought it was lovely. Once Mark laid the carpet down in the living room with the help of our neighbor, our collie walked in the living room and as soon as his four feet hit this lovely white carpet, his whole body quivered. He must have thought it was white grass because right then and there, he baptized it!

At one auction, Mark bought a huge and very heavy, cast-iron farm bell. After he had positioned it on a tall pole outside our back door, it proved to be quite handy for us. When the girls would be playing all over the countryside and I didn't know where they were, I would just ring the bell and they would appear. Even our collie Buddy knew ringing the bell meant business. Our neighbors would laugh and tell me that they never saw our dog anywhere, but as soon as the bell rang, out of the blue there was a streak of lightening crossing their backyard headed towards our house. It was our dog Buddy knowing it was time to eat!

However, there was still this looming sense of the need for a china closet hanging over me. I had lovely Tiffany crystal I had purchased before we were married and a set of china dishes; all of which had been packed in a box and unused for over 10 years. It would be nice to have them on display to enjoy and to use. I would go to different auctions and come back without buying anything because I felt the china closets I saw at these auctions always sold for more money than I thought we could afford.

I came home quite discouraged one day and confided in Mark as to how I was feeling. I asked if he would go along with me the next time to help me decide whether the cabinets I was bidding on were too expensive for us or not. He agreed to do this so when the next auction was scheduled, we took off to see what was available. I sat in the background and let him do the bidding and didn't pay much attention to what was going on. Another lesson learned: don't allow yourself to be passive when your husband is shopping at an auction! Mark's obsession kicked in again!

When the auction was over, he came to where I was sitting and gleefully announced that he had bought THREE china cabinets! Oh Gawd, I wanted to cry! Where on earth were we going to put all those china cabinets?

When we got home, we did a lot of shuffling around and somehow managed to have a china cabinet in three different rooms on the first floor. Then Mark felt it was his duty to fill all these cabinets with items he would bid on at different auctions.

Among some of these chosen treasures, were old ceramic urinals and bedpans! Yes! That last sentence is plural! This was getting out of hand! In fact a woman who stayed with our children when we went to a convention one time, told me when we came home that she called a friend of hers to tell her there was a piss pot in every china cabinet in every room on the first floor of the house!

Chapter 20

Always Expect
the Unexpected

We had lived in the farmhouse about a year when I decided the inside of the cupboards needed to be cleaned. Every once in awhile, I would see an ant crawling around and would get rid of it, but I didn't think much more about it. I reasoned that ants were insects that always seem to get into homes during the spring season. I did think the ants were somewhat larger than I was used to seeing though.

As I was removing the dishes from the shelves in the cupboard one day, I noticed a few more ants than usual and they were HUGE! As I checked them out a little closer, one ant stood up on its hind legs and stared straight at me!! No lie! That did it! No ant was going to try to start a fight with me! I saw a large hole in the wall at the corner of the shelf, which I figured had to be where the ants were coming from. I found a can of insect spray and sprayed the heck out of that opening! Ants were bygones forever in ant heaven! Buddha would have been very disappointed in me!

We had lived in the farmhouse about two years when Mark decided he needed to replace the flooring in the kitchen and also level the floor while he was at it. This was a wonderful idea I thought! The kitchen floor was so slanted that when a glass of milk spilled on the kitchen table, the milk never stayed in one place, but rolled onto the floor before anyone could stop it.

He suggested I take all the children to visit my parents in Pennsylvania while he tackled this project. Another great idea I thought!

After we were gone almost a week, I called Mark to tell him I planned to drive back home the next day. He suggested I stay a few days longer because he still wasn't finished and he really needed the time to complete this project. I agreed to this but thought it was quite out of character for Mark, since on other occasions when I would be away, he was always asking when I could come home or if I could come home sooner than I planned.

Once he gave me the OK to drive back home and I came inside the house, I saw what he had been doing; he had also decided to make a long harvest table for the kitchen out of wood he had purchased over the winter. He had left this wood in one of the sheds until he had time to get to it, and with all the temperature changes, the wood had warped. He had spent a considerable amount of money for the wood so he didn't want to scrap it. Instead, he decided to salvage it by smoothing it out with a heavy-duty sander.

Now our kitchen's wainscoting cupboards were built from the floor to the ceiling and had latches on them that didn't always allow the cupboards to close securely. So as he was sanding the wood, the doors kept opening one after the other and sawdust from the sanding would fly into the cupboards all over everything and into the nearby rooms on the first floor. As a result, when I came home I had the task of cleaning sawdust from almost everywhere on the first floor of the house and removing everything from all the cupboards to clean them before they could be used. The new flooring was very nice but the floor still slanted (not as much though.) I guess you can only do so much to repair a one hundred year old house.

Now we had a new kitchen floor but the walls in the kitchen were still papered with wallpaper that was quite dated. Mark's sister and family had just left after stopping by to visit us on their way to Maine, and were to be gone a week or so before they returned to our place again on their way back to their home in Ohio. I decided that would be a good time to get new wallpaper for the kitchen.

After choosing the wallpaper and checking the condition of the kitchen walls, I knew I was going to have to strip the old wallpaper before I could add any new. I had never papered walls before, other than when I used to help my mother at various times when she papered the home I grew up in. I felt I was being quite adventurous.

A mixture of vinegar and water was mixed in a spray bottle and I started to spray it on the wallpaper. Once the wallpaper was soaked enough to start peeling, I gasped! I counted 12 layers of wallpaper to be stripped before I could even consider beginning to do any papering! It seemed I had spent days of stripping wallpaper before I could even begin to prep the walls to repaper them!

Finally this goal was achieved and I started to do the papering. Then the phone rang. "Hello? Oh, you left Maine early and are headed back home? Oh, great! We'll see you then for dinner this evening?" Whoa! Pressure, pressure, pressure! Hurry, hurry, hurry! Finish getting the wallpaper on! Clean the mess from all the stripping! Figure what to have for dinner for four more people! Awgh!

I had just finished papering and cleaning the mess up after myself when they all walked in! I thought I was going to collapse! However, they suggested a brilliant idea!

"Do you know of a good restaurant in the area? We would like to take you out to dinner," my brother-in-law and sister-in-law said. Well, we just happened to know a great restaurant and it wasn't too far away! We all knew the kids would be happy with hot dogs and hamburgers at the house; and so it was. After that, when there were rooms that needed to be papered, I hired a professional to come and do the job.

Then there were the cluster flies, which my sister called dizzy flies. They seemed to be just a shell of an insect and all they did was spin around for a while, then drop over and die! We had never experienced such insects in western Pennsylvania, nor did we have them when we lived in Rochester. They were quite annoying and were endless in number!

I was first introduced to them the first winter on the farm when they started to appear around the bedroom windows upstairs. As the years went by, I discovered this always happened when the winter days got warmer and sunnier towards the end of the months of January and February.

It was awful!   I would go to the second floor and spray and spray around the windows until I was almost as dizzy as the flies. The spraying would leave a rug of dead flies that needed to be constantly vacuumed day in and day out to destroy any evidence of the massacres I participated in daily.

Chapter 21
Guest Fests

Everyone that knew Mark or I, was excited to see the farm. There was one particular day where we had cars in our driveway from three different states! They were all people who had decided to just drop by to see us and view the farm as they were passing through.

Until I spoke to Mark later, I figured they arrived by sonar or radar, because I never remembered giving them directions to our place nor did I know they were arriving.

Mark did admit one time that he told people at the office as he was leaving on Friday afternoons, "If you don't have anything to do over the weekend, come on down to the farm!" I really would have appreciated knowing this tidbit of information beforehand so I could be a little more prepared.

I would always try to have a couple pounds of ground beef handy for the family, but as the cars continued to pull in the driveway, I continued to make the ground beef patties that were to be grilled, smaller and smaller in size.

On one occasion I had a plate of hamburger patties ready to be grilled and I took the plate outside and set it on the picnic table for Mark to grill. I then rushed back in the house to continue to prepare food for the indefinite amount of people that were arriving.

At the time, Mark was talking to his boss and he never saw the neighbor's dog jump up on our picnic table and eat half of the meat on the platter! When I unexpectedly saw this happening, I panicked and screamed at the dog! There were a few choice words also exchanged between Mark and I over that one! I think that may have been the day I made the sign of the cross over the food I had available, with the intent and hope it would multiply like the loaves and fishes did so many years ago.

During those years we had a Volkswagen bus. This was extremely accommodating for us when we had visitors and we all ran out of conversations. We could always suggest we take them for a tour of Letchworth Park. The bus had enough seating in it to include another family. For those who aren't familiar with Letchworth, it is a beautiful State Park that is dubbed "The Grand Canyon of the East". Everyone that visited us was pleasantly surprised and happy to be on the tour.

Chapter 22

Parent's Prerogatives

My in-laws visited us on the farm more frequently than I thought they would. They were able to visit us the first November we lived on the farm, which was right after Tommy was born. My mother-in-law was quite taken with our baby boy and truly enjoyed being with him.

They came again to visit us the following spring to see their new grandson. While they were visiting, Mark's boss thought it was an opportune time to also visit and announce to Mark that he was promoted to become National Sales Manager. I was quite proud of him. However, as great as the promotion was, it meant a lot of traveling for Mark, which meant there would be no help on the farm other than the two older girls while he was gone.

Sadly, we hadn't lived on the farm for more than a year when my mother-in-law became ill and died, which left my father-in-law quite distraught. He lived two hundred and fifty miles away from us. Months later when Mark called his Dad, he could hear in his voice that he wasn't feeling very strong so he decided he needed to check on him. After driving to his home town, Mark discovered his father wasn't eating or sleeping much at all and for this reason was quite weak. Mark persuaded him to pack his things and come live with us for a while.

Then the fun began. When my mother-in-law was alive, my father-in-law expected three *hot* meals a day *plus* a decent bedtime snack. I tried to do this but I also had my family's needs to take care of as well.

I remember one time I was preparing a dinner of roasted turkey breast, mashed potatoes, gravy, vegetables and a salad. To save time, I didn't stuff the turkey breast, as I didn't feel we needed the extra carbohydrates, especially when I was making gravy and we had potatoes as well.

I guess this dinner wasn't the kind of dinner my father-in-law appreciated, because all during dinner he kept saying over and over again, "turkey without stuffing, turkey without stuffing, turkey without stuffing!" He may not have been happy about not having stuffing with the dinner, but I knew this dinner was still far better than the dinners of cold cereals he was eating at his home before he arrived here.

While he was living with us, every now and then he would give me extra money to "buy some REAL milk", he would say. (I would have 2% milk for the family because I felt it was healthier, but I guess he didn't feel that pertained to him.)

Every now and then he would also give me money to buy him these King Edward cigars. Ugh! What an odor! At times, the odor made me so sick and bothered me so much, that I was very close to threatening Mark that if his Dad continued to smoke the cigars in the house, it would have to be either his father or me to leave. However, I never had the courage to say this.

As the weeks went by, my father-in-law got stronger and happier. Before I knew it, he was up on the farmhouse roof helping Mark patch up some roofing and he was up and down ladders helping Mark paint the house. When Mark was at work or gone on trips, I would take my father-in-law for rides in the countryside to get him out of the house.

There was one occasion while Mark was on a business trip, that I decided that it would be fun to take my father-in-law and the kids to the Buffalo Zoo, which was an hour away. We had a good time, but time got away from me and we were gone longer than I planned. I knew my father-in-law felt he needed his cooked meal for dinner before it got too late in the day. When we got home, I threw together a bunch of stuff that I felt would make a quick hot meal and it was ready in twenty minutes! Mark's dad was quite shocked by that and I was even surprised myself!

My father-in-law and I really got along quite well but it got a little testy in the evenings after the 11 o'clock news was over and he would tell me it was time for me to go to bed. Excuse me? I had to nip that one in the bud right away!

Chapter 23
A Wee Bit
of Imbibing Time

The neighbor that rented our land to farm visited us one day to introduce us to their home brew of Dandelion wine. Well now, that was pretty special!! Once he saw that we enjoyed a little consumption of the liquid gold, he would stop by periodically and give us another bottle.

One evening while Mark was away on a business trip and it had been a long day for me, I decided to have a cocktail before I went to bed. I went to the cabinet where the spirits were stored and added some ginger ale to the alcohol. It tasted mighty fine. When I got up to go to bed, I went to refill the ice cube trays before putting them back in the freezer and the strangest thing happened. Every time I put an ice cube tray in the freezer, my body seemed to spin around quickly but the ice cube tray stayed in one place! I filled another tray to take to the freezer and the same thing happened! I stood there trying to figure out why this phenomenon was occurring.

The only recourse was to check the items in the cabinet. I picked up the ginger ale bottle that I had used to add to my drink and low and behold, it was Dandelion wine! Evidently when the neighbor dropped off a bottle for us one day, he put the 'home brew' in the ginger ale bottle and I was totally clueless of this. I don't know what the percentage of alcohol was in that home brew, but I know it had to be more than 13 per cent! I was amazed I was able to walk to bed that night!

When Mark was promoted to National Sales Manager, he traveled more than usual and became worldlier, so to speak. He would sometimes come home from a trip and introduce us to different exotic drinks that he became exposed to. One of those drinks was called a Black Russian.

One week my mother and grandmother were visiting us to monitor the kids while Mark and I had to go to another convention. When we got back from the trip, we were all together in the kitchen one evening, so Mark suggested that we all try this Black Russian drink. We eagerly accepted the offer.

After tasting the drink, both my Mom and grandmother thought the drink was wonderful, especially since they were practically raised on coffee. After they finished, Mark asked if they would like another one. My grandmother quickly said she would. So she drank the second Black Russian. After that, my grandmother became very quiet. Then she announced to everyone that she thought she might go to bed.

When they stayed with us, my grandmother and Mom slept in the little bedroom upstairs that was off from the back stairway by our kitchen. As my grandmother started to go up the first few steps, she backed down the steps again and peeked around the corner of the doorway to see us still sitting in the kitchen and very musically sang, "I'll-see-you-in-the-morning!" She never lived that one down and it instantly became our family anthem.

Chapter 24
Hurricane Agnes
Flood of 1972

W e had been on the farm for a year when it started to rain one day in June and it seemed to never stop. We had heard of Hurricane Agnes coming up the east coast but didn't think much about it, as we were way out of the proximity of the hurricane. Mark continued to drive back and forth to work as he always did. After four to five days, I heard on the news that the floodwaters from the hurricane were heading north and the Genesee River was involved. The Genesee River is one of the few rivers in North America that flows northward instead of south.

The Mt. Morris Dam was not too far from where we lived. The dam is at the northern tip of

Letchworth Park and the Genesee River runs directly through it. The dam is instrumental in keeping the river from flooding the outlying area.

I heard on the news that there was so much rain that the dam was almost to the point of overflowing. Most of the time, the water level behind the dam was no more than a little stream or creek. Because of my concern, I called Mark at work. He said they were on the alert at his company since they were on the east side of the river. If the dam overflowed, he and many others would either be in great danger or he might never get back to the farm for God knows how long!

I started to pace around the house again. The news was now telling us that the engineers were trying to let some of the water out of the dam but there was a glitch in the system. We were told that at the time the dam was built in 1950, the construction wasn't as sophisticated as it would have been if it had been built in 1972. The wheels that needed to be turned at the dam to let the water out had to be done manually. This is where the problem rose; they couldn't turn the wheels! This never needed to be done before, so things were a little rusty! However, I was grateful to learn that Mark was leaving work to get home as soon as possible.

Once he got to the farm safely, we got in the car and drove to the dam to see what was happening. I could not believe my eyes! The water was about 6 inches or so from the top of the dam and in danger of overflowing! I was amazed at the sight as this dam is 1000 feet across and 250 feet deep. All the way in back of the dam, as far as you could see, was water and devastation! We just prayed that the engineers would correct whatever problem there was regarding opening the valves to let the water out. If all that water overflowed, the whole Genesee Valley would be flooded as well as all of downtown Rochester. There would have been mass destruction and devastation everywhere.

We then drove down to the southern end of Letchworth Park. (The Park is 17 miles long). Once we got there, I couldn't believe my eyes! In between the two large waterfalls at the lower part of the Park, were parts of houses, roofs, cars and trucks shooting past us so fast in the river from the intense flow of the water, that I literally got dizzy when I turned to look away! The ground just seemed as though it was spinning around underneath me!

After we had driven back home, we heard on the news that the engineers were finally able to open the gates of the dam and allow the water to exit at a safe flow. Needless, to say, I was quite relieved and elated. We had so much rain by then that I noticed for a long time afterwards, there were no birds singing. I thought maybe all the rain and water might have drowned most of the birds and their nests. It was quite sad.

When I read the past history of this event, they said there was possibly over sixteen inches of rainfall around that time in Wellsville, NY. Wellsville is an hour south of where we lived and most likely where the flooding of the Genesee River originated.

Chapter 25
A Bit of Farm Freedom

Before we bought the farm, we had a small travel trailer that we used on camping trips. However, once we had the farm, it kept us so occupied we couldn't even think of going on a week or even on a weekend camping trip. We discovered in New York State that if you had a camper, whether you used it or not, you had to pay insurance on it to just sit on your property. I don't remember this being the case where we lived in Pennsylvania. We felt it was futile to pay insurance for something we weren't using anymore, so we sold the camping trailer.

After the trailer was sold, one afternoon Mark came home and told me that a friend of his had offered to let us stay at his cottage for a week on Martha's Vineyard. This sounded very exciting since I had never been to Martha's Vineyard before. Just the thought of having to take a ferry to the island made it seem even more exciting. So we decided to accept the friend's offer.

However, we had all the animals to consider. They definitely couldn't be left alone and the neighbor that was farming our property had more than his share of responsibilities with his own work, so we didn't even consider asking him to add anything extra to his workload. Instead, Mark decided to ask his father to come and help feed the animals on the farm. Mark felt this was a natural thing to do since his father had taken care of horses in the Calvary in World War I. His Dad said he would be happy to help out. His Dad also thought it would be a great experience for his sister to go along with him and see the farm.

As I was packing for the trip, I noticed one of the kids had left the large freezer door open. We kept this freezer on the back-enclosed porch. The ice was a good two to three inches thick on the shelves and on the door when I discovered this. I was very upset and wondered how I would have time to defrost all of this before we left. I decided to let it go until we got back because no one would be using the freezer while we were gone anyway.

Well, little did I know that my father-in-law noticed the ice buildup in the freezer and took it upon himself to defrost the freezer while we were gone. When we came home, my father-in-law was tickled to death with what he had done for us! He not only was excited to show us the job he had done on the freezer but he was also very excited to let me know *how* he did it! He did this amazing job—WITH A BLOW TORCH!! Quite the ingenuity, he thought!

How does one show another person appreciation for such a job well done, I thought? I thanked him but I almost choked on the words.

Chapter 26
The Call to Ireland

Mark came home one afternoon and excitedly announced that he was asked to go to Ireland for two weeks on business. This was a great opportunity for him. I went into a panic mode but wouldn't admit it to either myself or to Mark, especially when I knew how excited he was. It took me several years or so afterwards to understand how my not admitting things to myself affected my health.

How was I going to take care of all four children, a horse, three cows, the litter of dogs, etc., etc., all alone, while he was traveling those two weeks? Before I knew it, I contracted something that affected my heart. Just about every time my heart would beat, my whole body shook.

After seeing a local doctor for this strange experience, she told me to take Benadryl when I would feel this coming on. When I asked how much I should take, she answered, "as much as you need to stop you from feeling the way you are feeling." I did this until I took so much I could hardly function.

When Mark saw how I was being affected by this, he insisted that I see a doctor in Rochester that he knew and highly respected. When the doctor saw me, he checked me over and then began to ask me some questions.

One question he asked was, "Do you have time for yourself?" I responded that I did. He asked what it was that I did for myself.

I said, "If I get tired, I take a fifteen minute nap in the afternoon." The doctor said, "No. I mean *time for you*." I wasn't exactly sure what he was referring to.

He asked me if I ever got a chance to get out of the house on my own. I said "No."

He asked if Mark and I ever go anywhere alone together. I responded, "No."

He asked, "What does Mark do?" I told him that he and others at the company have been busy launching a new product. He gets home around 1:00 a.m. and gets up at 6:00 a.m. to go back to work which leaves no time to do anything or to go anywhere.

The doctor said that it was very important for me to have some time for myself.

After I had driven the hour drive back home, Mark met me at the door before I could get in the house. He had an inquisitive look on his face and asked me what the doctor had to say. I told him he said I needed to get out and have some time for myself. Mark's face showed both surprise and embarrassment.

Later that week the test results came back showing that I had Barlow's Syndrome or a mitral valve prolapse. After that, Mark decided we should make a point to go out to dinner once a month. And we did. And it was good.

Another lesson learned. Our nervous systems can do some strange things to our bodies that we can't always recognize. It's important for good health to have a balance in your life no matter what situation you are in. It is also important to understand your feelings and to be able to express them in a constructive manner.

Chapter 27
New Offering
In the Offing

As I mentioned before, Mark received a promotion as a National Sales Manager while we lived on the farm. He did very well at this new assignment. Well enough that within a couple years, he was promoted again to an assignment in Philadelphia where the company's main headquarters was located.

Naturally, Mark wanted to improve himself, so he accepted the offer. However, the girls had made enough friends during the four years we lived on the farm and they loved having the animals around so much that it was quite difficult for them to accept the move and the promotion their father received. There were many tears shed and vows made that one-day when they were adults; they would buy their own farm!

We also had to sell the animals before we left. It was pretty tough to watch Melissa the horse in the back of a truck drive down the road towards her new home after someone else bought her.

We accumulated so much over those four years because we had the room for it all. Now, it was time for us to hold our own auction. There was no way we could find and afford a home in the Philadelphia area large enough to keep all that we purchased at those auctions while we lived on the farm.

The next challenge was to find a home in one of the Philadelphia suburbs so it would be easier for Mark to travel to work and for me to be handy to doctors and hospitals when the family needed them. As before, it was quite discouraging at first but towards the end of the week we found a home that we both really liked. We put an offer in on the home and the offer was accepted. It wasn't long before we were on the road again moving south to Bucks County, outside of Philadelphia, Pennsylvania and onto another new adventure!

Chapter 28

Revisiting the Farm

40 Years Later

As I was getting towards the end of writing this book, I decided to see if I could reconnect with the present owners and hopefully be able to go back to the farm. I thought it would be a good idea to take some photos of the place and possibly use a photo of the farm for the book's cover.

When I called the owners, I left a message and the wife returned my call. She was very gracious and she happily consented to have me visit them. Since more than forty years had passed since we lived there, I wasn't sure what to expect. It was interesting to see the changes:

First of all, the 3-seated outhouse that was attached to the farmhouse was 'no more'! The wife told me that was one of the first things she put her foot down about! It had to go! I had to chuckle to myself over that one.

The side porch where the front entrance to the house existed was now an enclosed porch and that was nice to see. The back enclosed porch or washroom, was removed and in its place was an outside patio.

The ditch that Tommy accidently drove into with the VW bus when he was very young is now all filled in with a drain pipe underneath it. Some trees have been removed on the property and other newer trees have been planted.

They must still experience those horrific winds because when the present owner and I went up to the barns to take photos inside, we had to struggle to open the main barn doors at the top of the hill. They now have huge heavy metal doors that are supported with large wood beams and heavy cement stones to keep the doors from blowing off and away.

Once we were inside the barn, I looked for the cathedral ceiling that had impressed me the most when I first saw it. Instead, what I saw was a shallower room with the same type of ceiling. I think the present owners must have added a second floor to that part of the building. I meant to ask if that was the case but I forgot. If they did add a floor, I can see where it certainly would have given them much more space for storage or for anything else.

The magical gardens are all gone. The owner told me the farmers that plow the land for them now have machinery that plows the grounds wider and faster so it was beneficial for them to remove the gardens to help them achieve this. I also noticed the 10-acre hickory nut grove had also vanished and so had the lane that led up to it. All of this had occurred for the same reason.

Another Lesson: Nothing stays the same. Things are *always* changing.

And last but not least, I don't think there is any more evidence of the town dump!! They may have decided over the years to fill that in.   I forgot to ask the owner about that also!

EPILOGUE

There were many other experiences that the children and I remembered while living on the farm, but I didn't feel it would be appropriate to write about them.

This little book just contains a brief overview of what I remembered, and what rang the clearest in my mind during that time of my life.

Looking back over those four years, I felt the two older girls seemed to benefit more from living on the farm than the two younger children simply because of their ages. Their education in regards to the needs, schedules, and the routines of animals, how to plant and harvest food, how to preserve this food, and how to improvise in situations when other tools weren't available, all became an education they could never have experienced if they had lived in a town or city. The responsibilities and discipline they were forced to practice because of the animal's constant needs was an education they would never have learned in school. This can be taught, but until one needs to put it into practice, it is a whole different ball game.

The two younger children were too young to learn all that their older sisters learned in those years, but they still acquired an interest in growing vegetables, flowers, and trees, which have also benefited them greatly. Charlotte must have observed more than I realized because she and her husband plant a garden every year and she also cans and freezes the food every year. Tom presently has over an acre of land on a hillside in California where he has diligently and lovingly planted many unique and rare fruit trees for his family to enjoy.

I'm sure those who have spent all their lives from generation to generation, living on a farm and doing all the farm duties required, take this all in stride. It is a little different when a person goes into that kind of situation as a 'newbie' or rookie.

Looking back, it was traumatic at times, chaotic, frustrating, and a lot of hard work. However, no one learns anything by sitting around and allowing everything to be handed to them! *Amen!*

SOME RECIPES

Here are a few recipes for quick and simple meals that Peg prepared while living on the farm that helped her through some tight spots. These recipes are also included in her cookbook Rush Hour Recipes of America.

BAKED ACORN SQUASH AND SAUSAGE

Preheat oven to 350 degrees

1, 2, or 3 medium size acorn squash cut in half (depending on amount of people to feed.)
1 lb. of your favorite sausage
Salt and pepper to taste

Remove seeds from cut squash. Fill cavity of squash with pieces of sausage. Add salt and pepper to taste. Place the filled squash cut side down on baking sheet or dish.
Bake in 350 degree oven for 1 hour until squash is tender when pricked with a fork.

VEGETABLE MEDLEY CASSEROLE

Preheat oven to 325 degrees

16- 20 oz. bag of frozen vegetables, cooked and drained
16 oz. can small whole onions.
½ pint sour cream
½ cup small curd cottage cheese
½ teaspoon marjoram
½ teaspoon salt
1 tomato thinly sliced
¼ cup Parmesan or Pecorino grated cheese

Combine first 6 ingredients and mix lightly. Spoon all ingredients into buttered or vegetable sprayed casserole. Top with tomato slices and sprinkle with grated cheese. Bake in preheated 325 degree oven for 20 minutes. Serves 6-8.

LEFTOVER CHICKEN CASSEROLE WITH SHERRY

Preheat oven to 350degrees

2 or more cups cooked chicken broken into pieces
1 cup sour cream
1 can low sodium cream of mushroom soup
4 oz. can mushroom pieces
1/4 cup cooking sherry
8 oz. dry noodles cooked and drained
1/4 cup grated Parmesan or Pecorino cheese

Combine all ingredients except cheese and pour into casserole. Sprinkle top of casserole with cheese. Bake covered in preheated 350 degree oven for 30 minutes. Bake uncovered for additional 10 minutes.
Serves 6.

BROCCOLI AND NOODLES

Large saucepan of boiling water
8 – 16 oz. uncooked noodles (depending on amount of servings needed)
4 cups fresh broccoli cut in pieces
6 medium size fresh mushrooms cut into pieces or 4 oz. can sliced (optional)
Season salt
Parmesan or Pecorino grated cheese

When water comes to boil in saucepan, place desired amount of noodles, fresh broccoli and mushrooms in boiling water. Cook until noodles are done and broccoli is of desired tenderness (about 7 minutes.) Drain in colander and place in serving dish. Toss with grated cheese and Season Salt to taste. Drizzle olive oil or butter over top of dish if you desire (optional.) If you would like to use Angel Hair pasta or Capellini, cut or chop the broccoli into smaller pieces and cook pasta 5 minutes or according to past directions.
Serves 4-6.
Another idea: Cook spinach pasta and substitute cut up fresh cauliflower instead of broccoli.

Some house and barn photos: note the three seated outhouse attached to the farm house in second photo.

The barnyard before animals and fences were added.

One of the barn's majestic looking ceilings.

Tommy and Charlotte among the sunflower crop.

Tommy and Marie showing off the colored corn stash.

Tommy, with one of the favorite feral cats.

Melissa the quarter horse.

One of the German Wirehaired Pointer pups.

Marie and Terri, receiving their County Fair awards.

Biography

 Little did Peg Cleary-Osborne realize that a chance meeting with her friend would lead to another chapter in her life. As the two were howling over the verbal snapshots of life on a farm, her friend suggested she write a book and share them with everyone! Her friend felt that surely, there must be those who have never lived on a farm who would relish a peek into that life! Those who were in the thick of farm life may also enjoy the camaraderie!

As Peg thought about it, she knew she could weave through the process of getting a book published. After all, her cook book "Rush Hour Recipes of America" was a personal and financial success. She lived it! She often continues to dream about those days, so why not!

Before she knew it, Peg was writing a book about some funny and sometimes harrowing experiences while living on a farm in the 70's in the southern tier of New York State.

Made in the USA
Lexington, KY
11 December 2014